MARK (MARCH 1980)

4.

Act

08/2

The Book of
The House

Ernest Benn Limited
London & Tonbridge

About this book

What is a house?

This book describes some of the many strange and not so strange ways in which people have chosen to make houses. Have you ever thought why Eskimos live in igloos, or desert-dwellers build with mud bricks? Do you know why some houses have sloping roofs or how electricity reaches our homes?

Early on, people decided that they preferred to live in groups; you can read about the very first settlements and why we began to live in cities. Today, large-scale planning makes an enormous difference to our lives. But do the planners always know what we want? You can see here some of the most modern architecture, and some of the oldest cities in the world; some of the buildings we feel proud of, and those which many people try to forget.

There are suggestions for making model towns, castles and even a space city, and you can find out how to build your own house outdoors.

How would you like to live in the future?

Great changes are always taking place in the world around us. Maybe, looking at this book, you will get some ideas about how to make a house; and perhaps you will even think of a completely new and better way to design your surroundings and the way you live.

Contents

A day full of houses

It all began late one summer afternoon. Danny was bored. He was staying with his cousin Philip. Philip was a couple of years older than Danny and he usually had all sorts of good ideas for things to do. But Philip had developed scarlet fever and was lying pale and miserable in bed. It is a sad but true fact that when people are ill, it is hard even to talk to them properly, let alone do anything interesting with them. A game of cards failed and Danny got up and went out. He felt angry at Philip for being ill, and angry at himself for being irritated. Altogether, it did not look as if the holiday was going to be a success.

"Where are you going, Danny?" called his aunt.

"Out," said Danny, "for a walk."

He was passing the entrance gates of the Park, when the idea came to him. The Park was a grand name for what was really a rather untidy, overgrown wood with a few deserted fish ponds on the edge. It was quite a scarey place, even in broad daylight and Danny and Philip had never gone further than the edge. But today he was bored, and he was in a mood to make things happen.

Quickly, he looked around to see if anyone was watching and he dived under the broken and rusty fence. After a while, he became more and more aware of the noise he was making. The wood seemed very quiet and he had a strange feeling of being watched. He stopped. Everything was very still.

"I think I'll go back," he said out loud, to reassure himself.

"No you won't," said a voice.

Danny turned quickly. There was no one in sight.

"Who's there?" he said, and his voice, which he had tried to make firm and unafraid, wavered a little.

Someone giggled, and there was a sound of rustling leaves. Danny looked up. On a wooden platform about thirty feet up in an old tree was a boy. He was pointing a stick at Danny.

"We've got you covered," he called down. "Don't try to escape."

A shower of dead leaves and twigs fell on Danny's head.

"Stop that!" he said indignantly. Now he could see who it was, he felt angry at being scared.

"I'm going down to see who he is," said another voice and after more rustling and shaking of the lower branches, a pair of brown legs appeared, followed by their owner, who was a small girl with black curly hair. She dangled for a moment and then jumped. Danny was impressed. The branch was at least seven feet off the ground.

"I'm Ellen," she said, after rubbing her hands on her dress. "Do you want to come up?"

Danny followed her up a carefully hidden rope, to the main branch leading off the trunk and then up to the platform itself, where three pairs of hands hauled them over the edge.

It was the best camp Danny had ever seen. He and Philip had sometimes made little shelters in the long grass at the bottom of their garden. But this was a proper house. It had a roof of polythene sheeting stretched over a rough framework made partly of branches, and partly of wooden poles. There were boxes for seats, a table and some cupboards full of interesting things like an army torch, balls of string, tin cups and plates, comics, maps, a compass, some ancient toffee, nails, a hammer, matches, a pair of binoculars, glue, pencils and even a tablecloth.

"I'm Jack," said the boy who had spoken first, "I live here. This is Tom and Martha."

Danny sat down at the table. He admired everything. And the more impressed he was, the more pleased and friendly Jack became. They sat drinking Coke, swaying ever so slightly in the wind, with a fine view over the rest of the wood.

"Did you make this yourself?" asked Danny.

Jack looked slightly put out. "Yes. Well, not exactly. I think the gypsies started it, as a sort of lookout post. But they always go away in the summer. We brought all the things up here."

Everyday after that, Danny went to the Park. There was a secret signal and when they arrived they had to give a special long, low whistle. Of course it was possible to see someone coming for miles from the tree, but Jack said it was necessary. He also said it was good to be up high because then you were out of the way of prowlers or wild animals. It was a bit like a castle really and they could defend it against anyone. Ellen told Danny that although Jack liked to pretend he actually lived there, he always did go home after the others. But it didn't matter. It was good to think that this actually was their home.

Sometimes they would explore the Park and Danny soon learned how to move through the trees as quietly as possible. It made them feel as if they belonged and they were very scornful of the few adults who did come crashing into the Park with heavy boots and loud voices. Once or twice they even got within a few feet of the baby rabbits playing in the roots of the beech trees without disturbing them.

Much too quickly as it seemed to Danny, it was his last day. Ellen suggested going to have a look at the fish ponds. It was strictly forbidden to play in there, but as Ellen said, looking wasn't playing. After lunch it was drizzling so Danny borrowed all the umbrellas he could find. He felt a bit guilty because he hadn't asked anyone if he could take them, and he had his uncle's cane-handled blue silk one that he usually took to the office. As he left, Philip called out to him from the bedroom, "Where are you going?"

"Fish ponds," said Danny.

"They'll be mad if they find out," said Philip, "and you'd better look after that umbrella. It's Dad's best one."

"O.K." said Danny and he shut the front door.

By the time he reached the fish ponds it was pouring. Jack had the bright idea of huddling underneath the umbrellas so they made a kind of hut.

"I wish we knew how to make a real house for this sort of weather," said Ellen.

Tom suggested making a house on stilts on the edge of the fish ponds.

"Don't be silly," said Martha, "the bank isn't safe."

"We've got an old table at home," said Tom. "We could use that."

Everyone thought it was a good idea and it was not long before Martha was as excited as anyone. They carried the table to the edge of the fish ponds. Then they pushed it in, so that the feet were standing in a few inches of water. Martha climbed on and dragged up two old garden chairs, and the plastic sheet from her brother's tent. Jack and Danny arranged the umbrellas. It had stopped raining, but they made a very fine roof. Ellen had some chocolate in her pocket too, and they huddled in their new camp, pleased and excited.

The table tilted. "Careful," screamed Martha.

"We're falling!" They all grabbed at each other as they slid, shrieking and laughing, backwards into the water. Then everything got very confused. Danny felt the water close over him, and he struck out for the bank. He could hear Martha screaming in a panicky sort of way, and when he shook the water out of his eyes, he saw her, a few yards out, flailing her arms.

Suddenly, there were shouts. Someone dived off the bank. It was Danny's uncle, and he reappeared a few yards off the bank, holding Martha, wet and frightened in his arms. The others had by now scrambled up the bank.

"Here's Dad," said Ellen. "He'll be mad about the table."

Jack looked uncomfortable. "He'll be mad about us being here too."

And they were right. There was a great deal of fuss and general grown-up crossness. Martha's Dad was there too, and he was angrier than all the rest, although it wasn't clear exactly why. After all, they were all right and it wasn't his table that was now floating a few yards off shore.

Then Philip arrived. "I thought you were supposed to be in bed," said Danny as they were hustled back to the house.

"Well, I am, really, but Mum wanted to go shopping and she went to look for Dad's umbrella, so I thought I'd better let you know. Then Mum came out after me, and she saw you lot on the bank. She went mad and rushed back to get Dad. And then everyone came out and forgot that I wasn't supposed to be there."

Later that day when everyone had calmed down, they were all allowed to go around to see Martha who was sitting up in bed. Danny's aunt had baked a big chocolate cake for them to take and they all sat around munching and discussing how they could all meet up again.

"We can can go back to the tree camp next holiday," said Philip. "Then we'll be like nomads, living in different places."

"Nomads?" asked Tom.

"It's someone like a Bedouin who travels all the time," said Philip.

But Danny wasn't listening to them any more. He was thinking of the camp and all the things they could do next year.

People live in many ways

1 This camel is in Africa, in Somalia, and it is carrying a tent. The tent belongs to the boy who is sitting on it. It isn't only his of course; it belongs to his father as well, but you can't see him. He is at the other end of the rope, guiding the camel. The tent is their home.

2 These are Bedouin tents and they are in the largest desert in the world, the Sahara. The Bedouin are shepherds who travel from place to place with their flocks. This camp is near the Ghardaia Oasis in Algeria. An oasis is a desert spring where travellers can drink and rest. Often, it is the only green place for many miles.

Nomads and their tents

When we talk about houses, we think of the ones we ourselves live in and don't remember that there are others very different from our own.

First of all, the builder has to think about the kind of building material he has at hand and whether the climate is hot or cold. He also has to think about the number of people who are going to live in the house and what kind of dangers they are likely to face: wild animals, bandits or just pouring rain. A lot also depends on the sort of work they do: are they farmers or fishermen; rich or poor; and do they live a settled life or are they always on the move?

Finally, of course, the kind of house depends on the imagination of the people who live in it.

A Bedouin lives in the desert. He is travelling nearly all the time, looking for fresh grazing ground for his animals. We call people who live like this nomads. Like a lot of other nomads the Bedouin lives in a tent, because it is easy to put up and take down. It is usually made from the skins of his goats. But there are many different kinds of tents. Some American Indians live in cone-shaped ones, while the Badjaos often live in tents on boats. And there are many more.

3 A whole family lives in one tent. This family is in Saudi Arabia.

4 The Badjaos from the Philippines often live in boats covered with tents. They are nomads of the sea.

1 This boy lives in a shelter made of branches and grass in Africa.

2 This shelter has been made by some nomads from Kerman, in Iran.

Huts and shelters

Some nomads don't even carry tents with them. They make little shelters of grass and branches and when they move on, they leave these huts behind. Often, these nomads live in the forest or scrublands because in hot countries there is plenty of grass and leafy branches for them to use. They don't have to worry about snow and ice either! They stay for a while in one place, living on wild fruit and vegetables and hunting animals. Then, when their food runs out, they move on in search of more.

The small pigmies and the African Bushmen are nomads like this. They move around in little groups. One of their camps usually has only five or six huts, built around a fire in a clearing in the forest. To build their huts, they first make a simple frame out of wooden poles and then they cover it with branches and grass.

This is the simplest way of building a shelter and people all over the world make huts like the ones you can see here.

1 These houses in the Wadi Dahr Oasis in the Yemen look rather like castles. A large and often quite wealthy family of Arab farmers lives in each one.

Houses and strongholds

Here are some houses for people who want to stay in one place. The ones in the picture look a bit like castles. That is because in many ways they *are* castles, or strongholds at any rate. The Arabs who live here know that desert bandits might come and steal their goods, or even their fresh fruit and vegetables, which are valuable in such a hot, waterless country.

These houses often have five or six floors and are built with bricks made of sun-dried mud and straw.

Inside there are rooms for eating, working and sleeping in, as well as rooms for keeping tools and granaries. (Do you know what a granary is? It's a place for storing grain.) The family usually lives on the first or second floor. The ground floors are storerooms or for keeping animals. On the top floor there is often a room especially for the men. Here they smoke and talk or discuss business. You can see a lot of these houses in countries such as Morocco, Algeria and the Yemen.

13

1 The floating city in the port of Canton, China. It is made up of little boats called *sampans* which are anchored on the river, not far from the sea. Fishermen and their families live under shelters on these boats.

2 A floating house in the Bay of Sausalito, California.

Floating houses

Everyone knows that fishermen have to live near water. But they usually build their houses on land. In some parts of the Far East however, there are a lot of fishermen who actually live on their boats. In the Chinese port of Canton, for example, the fishermen's floating houses (called *sampans*) are literally part of the city.

On the other hand, some people live on the water simply because they like it. They aren't fishermen, but they still live on their boats. Maybe they live on huge yachts and sail from port to port or maybe they live on a house boat moored in one of the many waterways.

3 Houseboats on a canal in Amsterdam, the capital of Holland. There are a great many canals in Holland so a lot of people can live like this.

1 A pile-dwelling in a beautiful lagoon in Polynesia. The palm trees are growing on the horseshoe-shaped coral atoll, or island surrounding the lagoon.

2 Children playing in a village of pile-dwellings in the Philippines.

Houses on stilts

Houses can also be made *above* the water, if people don't want to live on their boats. First, poles are driven into the bed of a lake or river. Then, a small platform is fixed on the poles and finally the hut is built on the platform.

These huts are called pile-dwellings and they were invented long ago by people who wanted to be safe from their enemies and wild animals. Look at the picture. If anyone was swimming to attack, the people in the houses could easily see them. There are people living in pile-dwellings in many countries.

3 This large village of pile-dwellings is on a lake in a West African country called Dahomey. Pile-dwellings as you can see, are built in shallow water, because it is difficult to make them when the water is deep.

Houses underground

Did you know that in prehistoric times, men sometimes used to live in caves? Today, there are still some people especially in hot countries, who live in caves. They make these caves into homes because the temperature doesn't change much in a cave. It is cool even in very hot weather and not too cold at night.

Some houses are even dug out of a mountain, like the village of Matmata in Tunisia. The villagers dug out enormous round holes to make a sort of courtyard, and then they made their houses in the steep sides of the hole. The courtyards were reached by a long, underground tunnel. In this way they were well protected against any enemies.

1 Here you can see the great holes where villagers of Matmata in Tunisia once dug out their homes. You can just see the doors and windows of their houses. There are stables and granaries as well as living rooms.

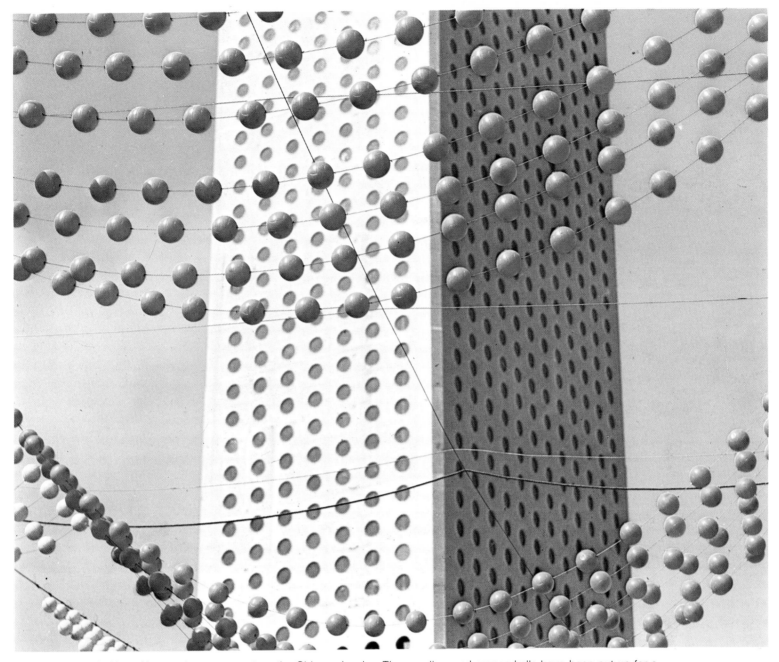

1 A skyscraper in Hong Kong, a huge sea port on the Chinese border. These yellow and orange balls have been put up for a festival. The skyscraper looks like something from a toy construction set, or maybe a bit of white pegboard. It certainly doesn't look very solid.

Skyscrapers

Everybody knows what a skyscraper is. It is a very tall building full of all kinds of offices and flats. Why did people begin to build them? It was mainly because the more men and women wanted to live in the city, the more difficult it became to find enough land on which to build. There seemed only one answer: to build upwards instead of outwards. But are skyscrapers the best way for people to live? They can be a little like huge cupboards with lots of tiny drawers. Inside, people live very close together, but that does not mean they know each other any better.

2 Skyscrapers on Manhattan Island in New York.

1 The Villa Barbero at Maser in the Veneto, Italy. In Italy, such rich and beautiful houses are called *villas*. This one was designed by a famous architect called Andrea Palladio. All over Europe, people tried to copy his style of building. He loved elegance and grace and he tried to make his buildings look well balanced — do you like it?

Country houses

Rich people are often lucky enough to choose where they want to live: in the country, by the sea, or in the mountains. And through the centuries, they have built many beautiful houses and palaces all over the world. For example, in England there is Longleat and Windsor Castle. In America, there are mansions such as Monticello, in France, the chateaux of the Loire and in Italy the great villas of Tuscany and Veneto. The list is endless.

These rich people were able to encourage and support artists, musicians and sculptors. They created the fashions of their day and their houses are full of the lovely (and not so lovely!) things of their age. Today, the government and big companies as well as private individuals, are responsible for most of the biggest modern projects. Look around you at the new buildings. Which ones would you like to last for hundreds of years?

2 This strange building is an ancient palace in Kashan, Iran.

3 This is what it looks like inside. See how intricately it is decorated with gold and enamel.

Slum houses

Poor people have much less choice about where they live. In cities this often means they live all together in the least pleasant places. Sometimes this is on the edge of the city; but sometimes too it is in the middle: the forgotten areas of crumbling buildings, no lavatories and little or no lighting, heating or water.

All over the world, there are people who have to make their homes out of corrugated iron, bits of wood and even cardboard; or anything else they can find that has been thrown away. These places are often called slums or shanty towns.

Why do people come to these places? They are often even poorer in the countryside, and they come in search of work, hoping desperately for the chance to make a better life for themselves.

1 Shacks in a shanty town on the edge of Bombay, India.

2 A depressing sight. Shacks called *favelas* on the hills outside Rio de Janeiro, Brazil.

1 Maria painted this house with help from Barbara and Max. It is deep in the country in the middle of a field of flowers. Can you see that the windows are shut? That is to make sure that the children inside won't be disturbed.

2 Robert wrote about this picture: "I want to live by myself in a spaceship. My spaceship can travel on earth as well as in space".

What sort of a house would you like?

You have now seen how some people all over the world are living, but there are of course lots of other ways. Although it sometimes looks odd at first sight, especially if your own house is very different, there is usually a good reason why people are living the way they do. After all, they may have worked it out over hundreds of years. In fact, many people are very happy with the way they live.

But others are not so lucky. Perhaps they are not so poor as the people in shanty towns, but they are still a long way from living as they would choose. Do you like your house? Is there anything you especially like about it? What don't you like?

Perhaps you can't think of any way in which it could be improved. But if you *can*, why not invent a house of your own? That is what these children of 6, 7 and 8 have done.

3 Another Robert drew an enormous tree house.

4 Susanna wants to live here simply because she likes it.

5 Nina wants a floating house.

6 Nelson wants his house to be in the middle of a wood.

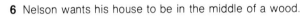

7 Sylvia, Rosamund and Josephine designed this house. Grown-ups are not allowed in it "because they make too much fuss".

8 Angela wants to live in an igloo and be allowed to do anything she wants.

21

On the farm

There are many folktales and legends about farms and property, because it was even more important a long time ago to have a good piece of land than it is today. It could make all the difference between life and death. This is a story, and many people say it is a true one, about a poor young farmer called Jed.

Jed was a cheerful person and he didn't let his lack of land make him depressed. His cottage was clean and bright and every morning he got water from his well and every evening there was milk from his cow. All in all, he considered himself quite fortunate.

He had two neighbours, both disagreeable, spiteful people, who spent most of their time comparing their lives with others more fortunate than themselves and generally making themselves miserable.

One evening, they began talking about Jed. Needless to say they hadn't a good word to say about him and they began thinking what a fine thing it would be if his land — which divided theirs — belonged to them both.

"All he has is the cow," said one.

"And if the cow happened to have an accident . . . " went on the other and winked, knowingly.

No more was said. But a few days later poor Jed woke up to find his cow very sick; and by the end of the week she was dead. Jed was heart-broken. Still, there was nothing to be done but to take her hide and sell it in the market. As he walked out of his gate he met his neighbours, who were smiling broadly.

"We thought we'd do you a good turn," said one.

"We'll generously offer to take the farm off your hands. We can see you won't be needing it any more," went on the other. Jed looked sad. "I'll think about it," he said. Without his cow, he could hardly afford to live on his farm.

He went on down the road until he was passing by the house of the richest farmer in the county. In the garden, pegging out the washing was Sally, the farmer's daughter. Now Sally had a soft spot for Jed and when she saw him walking slowly up the road without his usual bright, warm smile, she called out to him and asked him what was the matter. After a little while Jed told her and she was full of concern and kindness.

"Come in," she said. "Father is away on business and Mother has been getting a big party ready for her friends." The farmer, who had a very short temper, hated to see his hard-won gold disappearing on entertainment and his wife would only give a party when he was safely out of the house.

Jed went in, and his mouth watered at the sight of all the good things laid out on the table: roast duck, roast chicken, roast turkey and whole batches of warm, new-baked bread; cakes, creams, syllabub, fruit, flagons of cider, cheeses and hams. There was everything anyone could wish for. They were all just about to sit down to the feast, when a servant rushed in, full of consternation. "The master's coming back! The master's coming back!"

There was pandemonium, as everyone tried to hide themselves. But Jed had an idea. "Listen everyone," he called. "Put the food where I tell you and then let me lock you all in the barn. And if you do what I say, there will be no need for alarm."

There was only just time to hide the food when the farmer walked through the door. He was hot, tired and hungry — and very disagreeable. His best horse had gone lame. His wife rushed up anxiously to ask if there was anything he needed. "Food," he said crossly, "and be as quick as you can. I haven't eaten since daybreak." His wife didn't know what to do. She could hardly bring him the feast — yet there was nothing else she had to offer. And say he saw the apple pie that was poking out from behind the dresser, not a yard from his foot? She looked upset. Sally looked confused and all the servants tried to make themselves as scarce as possible. "What is the matter with everyone?" demanded the farmer. Then he saw Jed.

"And what are *you* doing here?" Jed looked up calmly, holding his hide.

"I am talking to my cow," he said.

"Talking to your cow!" exploded the farmer. "Are you mad?"

"Not at all," said Jed, "and if you will calm down and speak gently to her perhaps my cow will think about bringing you something to eat."

The farmer was almost speechless with rage, but his anger soon turned to astonishment as Jed said, "My cow says there is roast duck in the flower pot." Sure enough, there was the roast duck. "My cow says," went on Jed, "that there is an apple pie behind the dresser." The apple pie was brought out; and Jed went on consulting his hide until the whole feast was on the table.

The farmer's eyes began to glisten at the sight, and after they had sat down to eat, he said very casually to Jed, "Ever thought of selling that cow? For a special price, of course."

"I might," said Jed, equally carelessly. "For a special price."

"Care to name it?" said the farmer.

"Your daughter Sally's hand, if she'll have me, and a purseful of gold," said Jed promptly.

The farmer was rather taken aback, but he reasoned it this way; obviously, Jed was a man who could provide for Sally, and his ragged clothes must be some sort of a disguise. Why, that feast they were eating was worth twenty suits of clothes. And the purse of gold? He would get that back in a week's meals, if they were all like this.

"Done," said the farmer.

Sally was watching in high glee and she ran off to pack. Jed handed over the hide and begged the farmer to treat his cow well.

"There is only one thing," he said with a grin.

"Sometimes she will invite guests to your meal as well. In fact, I think I can hear them already in the barn." With that, he and Sally rode off back to his farm.

When they arrived, they found his two neighbours, moving out all his things.

"Hey," said Jed. "I got such a good price for my hide that I'm not selling. The two neighbours stopped. "Yes," went on Jed. "Farmer Roberts wants cow-hide so badly that he gave me a purseful of gold for mine." The two neighbours looked at each other and with one accord they ran home to get all the hides they could find. Then they galloped off to Farmer Roberts' house.

You can imagine the confusion that was going on there: angry guests, the farmer's wife in hysterics, not to mention the loss of the purse full of gold. When the farmer heard that two strangers had arrived with cow hides to sell he simply picked up a big stick and thwacked them until they ran off howling.

It took some time for the dust to settle, but the farmer really was very fond of his daughter and she was so happy it was hard to dislike his new son-in-law, who was so cheerful and good-natured. In the end, he welcomed Jed into the family, saying that as Jed was the only man to have outwitted him, he was sure to be a good man to look after his property when he was no longer able to do so.

Once there was a castle . . .

2 Gustave Doré drew these towers as part of his illustration for *The Ancient Mariner* by Samuel Coleridge.

3 This castle is part of an illustration by Edmund Dulac from Hans Christian Andersen's *The Wind Tells of Waldemar Dae*.

Fairytale castles

Fairytales, myths and legends are full of castles: Sleeping Beauty fell asleep in a castle, Rapunzel was locked in a tower by a wicked witch and The Holy Grail in the King Arthur story was kept in an enchanted castle.

And castles, at least, are real. Long ago, kings, queens, lords and princes really did live in them. Of course, they did not all look like the castles in these pictures. These are imaginary castles and they all have a story.

In fig. 2, you can see the Ancient Mariner, wandering round the city telling people about his terrible voyage on an enchanted boat.

In fig. 3, a young princess is picking flowers close to the castle where she lives.

In fig. 4, the magic city you see here was built by an enchanted swan, when his life was saved by the son of a Czar and his mother.

4 The magic city painted by Jan Bilibin from *The Story of Czar Saltan* by Alexander Pushkin.

◁ 1 This fairytale castle opposite doesn't have a story. Why not make one up for yourself?

1 The Castle of Eltz, near Koblenz in Germany

2 Karatsu Castle in Japan is not far from the sea. It looks much more like a beautiful house than a castle.

Castles all over the world

Why did people live in castles? They began as places to protect those inside from enemies. The earliest castles were often simply a strong, wooden fence surrounding a few huts where the people lived. Outside the fence, there was normally a deep ditch to make it difficult for attackers. Later on, they were usually made of stone with a big tower (called a *keep*) in the middle. Many were built on hill tops or cliffs, so that they could command the countryside around and lords and princes had many soldiers living in their castles so you can imagine that they were very powerful people. Castles like these are built when life is uncertain and dangerous and when

3 Braemar Castle in Scotland has round towers.

4 Chillon Castle was built on the edge of Lake Geneva, Switzerland. You can imagine how desperate prisoners in there must have felt.

5 Castle Torrechiara, near Parma, Italy. This was first built as a stronghold, but later it was made into a beautiful palace.

6 Monastir Castle in Tunisia. This is really a monastery.

different leaders are at war with one another.

When times are more peaceful, rulers don't have to worry so much about their enemies and they are more interested in being comfortable. You can see this in the pictures here. Sometimes these palaces were marvellously designed and decorated with no expense spared.

In some wild and remote places in Africa and Asia, there are still lords who live in castles and have complete power over the people living round them. But on the whole, stone walls are no longer any use for keeping out invaders and we have to try to stop wars in more peaceful ways.

7 The fortress house of the Imam of Wadi Dahr, in the Yemen. The Imam is an important Moslem ruler.

8 Château Chenonceau, built on the River Cher, in France, looks more like a fairytale palace than a fortress.

9 The castle of Udaipur on Lake Pichola, in India.

2 This is a picture of Alnwick Castle, painted over two hundred years ago by an Italian artist called Canaletto.

Castles in pictures

If you really want to see what castles used to look like, you should look at old paintings. The Château of Vincennes has been altered since it was first built; but fig 3 shows the beautiful keep as it used to be. Can you see too the battlements on the walls and towers which protected the archers as they shot their arrows?

Sometimes, of course, a castle doesn't change much over the centuries; but anyway, it is fun to see what people wore and what they did in the past.

1 In this Indian painting, you can see a child playing with doves in the garden of a beautiful palace.

3 You can see the Château de Vincennes in Paris in this painting by Jean Fouquet. The castle was then a prison.

4 A procession of ladies-in-waiting in white in the wonderful palace gardens belonging to one of the ancient Chinese Emperors.

1 The old walled city of Carcassonne in France. Look at the towers in the walls which make them even stronger.

2 The ancient city of Jerusalem where David and Solomon once ruled, still has walls which were standing at the time of Christ.

The walls

Walls were built for defence. A long time ago, houses, villages, cities and even whole countries were surrounded by walls and people made them even stronger with towers and battlements.

Because of our modern weapons we need something stronger than just a wall today, but in lots of countries you can still see what is left of the old defences. Perhaps you have seen some yourself.

3 The walls of the ancient capital of the Incas, Cuzco, in Peru. Each block of stone was at least 3 m. wide.

4 The Great Wall of China was built by the Emperor Tsin. It is the longest wall in the world.

Sandcastles 1 Do you like making sandcastles? These two children are making towers in a special way by running sand and water through their fingers.

2 You can build all kinds of towers, temples and palaces out of sand. This one is rather like a Mayan pyramid. (See page 87).

Model castles

Throughout this book, the instructions for making things are meant to show you the *basic* methods. The most interesting part of building, of course, is when you invent your own special design and these ideas should only be the starting point for your own models. If you think, there are all kinds of things you could add to the polystyrene castle below; like a drawbridge you can raise and lower, men on horseback, trees or a well. You could even paint window slits in the towers, if you wanted.

When you are working, try to read through the instructions carefully first. Then you can collect together everything you are going to need. Unless you are lucky enough to have a workbench, cover the table where you are working with plenty of newspaper or cloth and be careful with sharp tools. Look ahead; once something is glued together it's sad to have to take it apart because you have left a bit out. And don't forget to clear up; it's easier to work if you can find what you need.

A castle of polystyrene 1 Use a knife to cut the polystyrene into squares and rectangles. Ask an adult to help with this.

2 When you stick the shapes together, make sure you have the right kind of glue for polystyrene.

3 The walls can be made from long rectangular pieces. Cut out a hole in the wall for your gateway. Cut out big square blocks for towers and little ones for battlements and glue them to the walls.

4 If you like, you can give each tower a big turret as you can see here. Now the walls are finished.

5 Next build the castle keep in the same way and put it inside the walls. The keep should be taller than the walls.

6 Now you can add anything else you want. This castle has a roof made from the two triangle-shaped pieces (see fig. 5).

Instant castle 1
From a hardware shop, or your friend's workshop, get a piece of polystyrene that has been used for packing equipment.

2 Choose a shape you like and begin your castle. You can add all sorts of things to the basic shape: wire, foil, straws, coins etc.

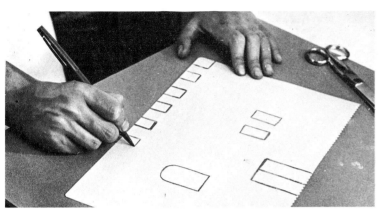

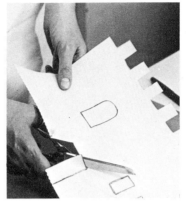

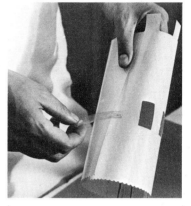

A card castle **1** Find a piece of thin card for your tower, and draw on it doors, windows and battlements as you want them.

2 Cut out the shape you have drawn. Do this for as many towers as you want.

3 Roll each tower into a cylinder and join the two sides with sticky tape.

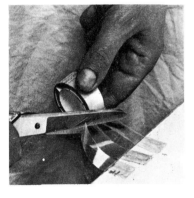

4 It's easier if you have the sticky tape ready cut and stuck to the edge of the table.

5 If you want a cone-shaped tower, take a piece of paper and holding it firmly in one hand, roll it up with the other.

6 Roll it more tightly towards one side until it comes to a point.

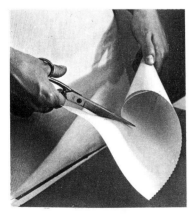

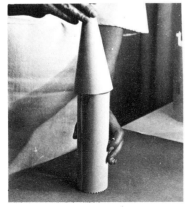

7 Next cut off the triangle-shaped flap of paper at the open end of your cone.

8 Stick the cone together with tape. Now fix it on top of your tower.

9 You can invent all kinds of towers. The walls stand up if you bend them at the corners to make a right angle. What else do you want to put in your castle?

The black castle

Many, many years ago there lived a king who had one daughter. She was as pretty as a sunny day in spring and the king loved her dearly. They lived in a large, stone castle and although there were troubles in those days as there are now, they were mostly very happy. Then one day the princess fell ill. The king was horrified; but there was nothing anyone could do and we can only imagine his sadness when she died and was laid beside her mother in the little churchyard. The king locked up the castle and sent everybody away.

Years passed, and no one came near the castle. Houses grew up around it, railways, factories and shops. All that was left in people's minds was the dim memory of some tragedy that had happened in the Black Castle, as they now called it. After all, they had plenty of sad things of their own to worry about. They had to work hard and there was little space to play.

In that town lived a boy called Dan. He and his friends had found a big patch of wasteland on the edge of the town. It had been an old dump and Dan was getting everyone to build a hut there. For the first time, they had somewhere of their own to play.

Then one day six bulldozers arrived and with them, lots of workmen. "Hop it, kids," said the foreman. "Why?" said Dan. "Because this is going to be a new housing development, that's why," said the foreman. "Sorry, but we can't have you running around everywhere."

The next day brought barbed

wire and a fence, and that was that. No more playground. Dan felt so furious and miserable that he couldn't bear to talk to anyone and he set off home by himself. He didn't much care where he went and he soon found himself near the Black Castle. It was getting dark by now and he sat on a stone, staring at the walls.

"I wish I'd lived in the Black Castle," he said crossly. "I bet children could play anywhere they liked in those days."

"Oh, but it wasn't always nice," said a soft voice close by his elbow.

"Who's there?" said Dan, trembling a little.

"You're not afraid of *me*, are you?" said the voice with a laugh.

"Of course not," said Dan, rather quickly.

"Well," went on the voice in a friendly way. "If you're not, why don't you come up to the castle? I've been so bored all these years playing on my own."

The next day Dan led a party of curious children up to the castle. They cleared up the cobwebs, explored all the rooms from the great, dark hall to the little bedrooms in the towers. There were hundreds of places to play and soon it was the most popular place in the whole town. Even some grown-ups came too, although only if the children asked them.

All this happened many years ago now, and I'm only telling the story as it was told to me. Myself, I think it was the princess who spoke to Dan. But he would never say. He said it was a secret.

What goes into a house?

Materials

People nearly always make their homes from materials which they can find around them. This has been true ever since prehistoric times. If early man lived in the forests, he made simple huts of branches and leaves to protect him from bad weather. And today, in some parts of the world, there are still people who make shelters in exactly the same way.

People like the Arabs or the Indians in America, who live in the desert, use bricks of **sun-baked mud to build their houses.** This is because there aren't many trees in the desert. Using the materials around you often has other advantages as well. They usually survive best in the climate you live in. For example, in the desert it is very hot in the day and cold at night and mud bricks can last longer in these extremes of temperature than reinforced concrete!

In fact, the bricks we use today are basically a sort of baked mud; although of course we have developed them to suit modern buildings.

2 This hut with its cone-shaped roof is called a *trullo*. It is in Puglia, Italy. It is built rather like an igloo, only with stone blocks instead of ice, which are put on top of each other in smaller and smaller circles.

3 A small igloo, made in winter by an Eskimo out hunting.

◁ **1** This beautiful painting is by the Dutch artist, Jan Vermeer. It is called *The Alleyway.*

4 This is a Laplander. See how warmly he is dressed. He is on his way to see that his reindeer are safe in their pen. In Lapland there are big forests, and as it snows a great deal in winter, the Laplanders build warm cabins out of logs. In the summer, when the weather gets better, some Laplanders are nomads and live in tents.

5 These huts made of maize-stalks are in Chad, in Africa. The woman is pounding maize grains into flour.

In the arctic forests of Northern Canada and Russia, people make log cabins because there is plenty of wood. It also keeps them warm in winter, when, as you can see from this picture of Lapland, it gets very cold.

In fig. 5, you can see a very different sort of house made with bundles of maize stalks. The people eat the maize they grow and use what is left over from the plant to build their houses.

In fig. 6, these Iranian peasants' houses are made with thick walls of baked mud and straw. This is because it helps to keep them cool in the day and warm at night. But most important of all, because it is the best building material they have.

6 These houses in Saltanich in Iran are made of sun-baked mud and straw. The straw on the roof is drying in the sun.

1 & 2 On this page you can see a very strange house made by a stone-breaker from Glenford, USA. It is an old car! Fig. 1 shows the front of the car house. He has decorated it with lots of little dolls — can you see? Fig. 2 shows the steps he has built leading up to his door.

You can make almost anything into a house

Yes, that is true; as long as it will stand firm and will not fall to pieces in rain, snow or wind. As you can see, it is even possible to live in a car. This man wedged his old Studebaker into the ground and built on anything he needed (like steps) with planks to make his home. But people also live in cars because they want to travel around. In some countries, you can still see gipsies, wandering from place to place in beautifully decorated caravans, just as they always did: although today, they tend to use more modern means of transport.

People often have to live in what they can find; an old shed, a deserted garage or factory or even a telephone box (although you would have to be quite small to live here). Sometimes it can be fun. You can make your house as you want it and it is your home and not just a shelter from the weather.

But it is one thing to choose a strange kind of house and quite another when people are forced to live in old boxes, or tumble-down shacks because they simply have nowhere else to go. Then it stops being fun and is a terrible way to live.

3 Here, you can just see the roof almost hidden in a mass of flowers.

Telephone house

1 Rita is looking out of the telephone box. She shouts, "This is our house! No one's to come in!" Kate, Martha and Tom are inside the telephone box too and they are all laughing.

2 How did they get there? They were all round at Tom's house, playing houses in the clothes cupboard. Tom's mother got very cross when she saw them and so they ran out into the street. Then Tom saw the telephone box and they all rushed inside.

3 "This is the best house in the world!" they shouted to everyone who went past. "It's even got windows in the door." They looked through the telephone directory and laughed at some of the funny names. Then they pretended to telephone. "Hello, hello. Is that Mr Nobody? I can't hear you. What a silly thing to say!"

4 Rita says, "I like this house much better than the cupboard house. No one is going to get us out!" And she peeks out of the door to see if anyone is coming.

5 There is! It's a policeman! "Quick! Run!" she yells as she rushes out giggling. "What's all this?" says the policeman. But he isn't really cross. Martha, Kate and Tom slip out too, and pretend they were coming out anyway.

6 Tom hitches up his trousers which are a bit too long for him and says "Kate, let's all go back to my place and make a house in the back garden." And they do.

Why not make your own house?

Many people live in cities, in big buildings built and designed by people they have never heard of, and who have certainly never heard of them. That is one of our big problems today. A lot of planners think they know what people *ought* to want. And sometimes it isn't what people want at all. There are planners who think that everyone would be happy if they all lived in the same way. In fact, a very

A bin house **1** Collect 30 empty detergent containers (or large cardboard boxes) from a supermarket and put a little sand in 10 of them.

2 Put 2 containers on top of one containing sand and tie all 3 together with wire. Do this with all your containers. Now you have 10 columns.

3 Make three walls out of the columns of containers, as you see here. Careful! The columns must stand firm. Make the roof out of a sheet of polythene.

A cardboard house **1** Find a large piece of packing cardboard, at least 1 m. high and 3 m. long. Fold it as you can see in the diagram. Cardboard is easier to fold if you score it first with a ruler or the back of a knife.

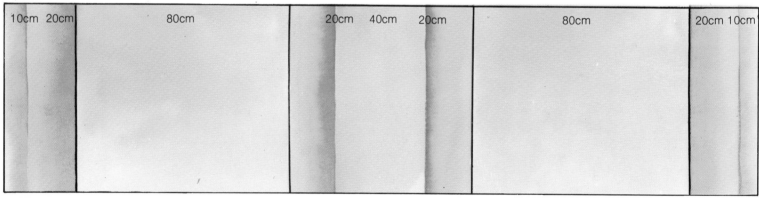

| 10cm | 20cm | 80cm | 20cm | 40cm | 20cm | 80cm | 20cm | 10cm |

2 You can change the measurements to suit your piece of cardboard, but don't forget that if the sides are too long, your house will be very narrow.

3 It is easiest to make the A folds first, then the B ones and so on.

4 Fix a sheet of polythene over the top for a roof, and cut out windows. Now your house is finished!

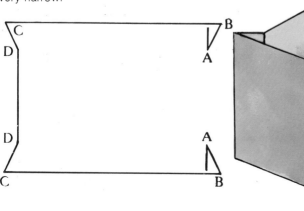

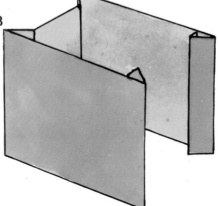

famous architect called Le Corbusier said he would like to see 'a single building for all nations and all climates'. Do you think that would be a good idea? Think about it.

Meanwhile, why not make a house yourself? Your building materials will depend on what you can find, but there are suggestions here for houses you can make in the city as well as ones for the country. Some of them are a bit complicated, so get some help from grown-ups. It is a good idea to ask them anyway, because you will need someone to help you check that your frameworks are firm.

A two-tree house **1** If you can find two trees close together, you can make all sorts of houses. First of all, you find a pole and tie it firmly to the two tree trunks. (This isn't as easy as it sounds!)

2 Now make two frames roughly the same size from poles or thick bamboo canes. (They don't have to be as complicated as the ones in the picture.) Make sure that they are long enough to reach from your pole to the ground.

3 Lean the frames against the pole, one on each side. Tie them tightly together. The frames now make the sloping roofs of your hut. Next, you have to work out a way to cover them.

4 If you can find them, you could use leafy branches and twigs, like the bushmen. This will make your house cool and fresh.

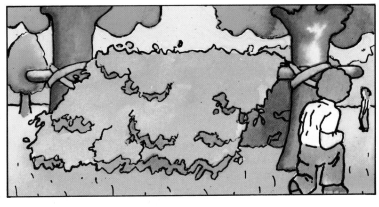

5 Otherwise you could use straw or hay, or even fresh-cut grass. Do check at this point that your horizontal pole is firm. It will be safest if you have rested either end on a branch sticking out before tying it.

6 If you have a large piece of canvas, you needn't bother with the frames at all. You can just put the canvas over the pole, fix the ends of the material to the ground with pegs, and you have a tent.

The framework   1 This must be strong because it has to hold everything up. Hammer poles firmly into the ground and jam them tightly with little pieces of wood. Get someone to check for you that they are firmly fixed.

2 If you are using pegs to hold the canvas in place, drive them in firmly too, and at a slant. They must keep the canvas taut, otherwise your tent will sag.

3 The houses and tents in these pictures are made with forked poles. If you can't find any, carve away a hollow at the end of an ordinary pole, fit another pole into the hollow and tie the two poles tightly together.

A house around a tree   You only need one tree for this house. If it has a low branch, tie the canvas to it very firmly. Then pull the canvas out into a circle and fix the ends into the ground with pegs. If there is no branch, you could hammer wooden poles lightly into the ground, and then push them until they are leaning against the tree trunk (making sure that they don't slip). Then you can cover them with canvas or straw.

A two-pole tent   1 Find two forked poles roughly the same length. Knock them firmly into the ground. (See above). Put a long pole on top of them and tie it tightly to the forks. Then hammer in two pegs at each end and stretch a rope tightly between the pegs and each fork, as you can see here.

2 Cover the pole with a large piece of canvas and fix it tightly to the ground with pegs. If you want a back to your tent and a flap at the front, you must measure and cut out another two triangular pieces of canvas and stick them on as you can see in the picture.

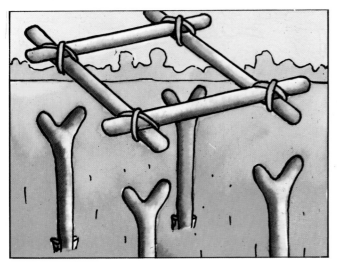

A four-pole house **1** Mark out a square on the ground, the size of the house you want to make. Find four forked poles the same length and hammer them firmly into the ground at the corners of your square.

2 Find four more poles, slightly longer than the sides of your square and tie them tightly together to make a frame. Check that your frame will fit on the forked poles, and then tie it firmly to the poles.

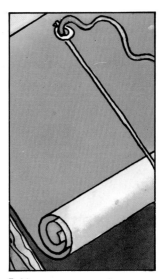

3 Cover two sides and the roof of your house with a large piece of canvas and then fix it firmly to the ground with pegs.

4 With another piece of canvas, cover the third and fourth walls. Peg the canvas at the foot of the third wall, and screw a ring through the canvas into the top of the frame of the fourth wall, which will be your door.

5 You can now make a roller door with some string.

A six-pole house **1** Begin your house as before by hammering in firmly four poles of roughly the same length. Then drive in two slightly longer poles, one at each end, so that they are facing one another across the square. Put seven more poles on the forked poles and then tie them on firmly. These make the framework for the roof.

2 You will need a very large piece of canvas to cover this house. Remember to fix it firmly to the ground all the way round. To make a back, cut out another piece of canvas and stitch it on. A flap for the front can be made in the same way. If you liked, you could cover this house with leafy branches or straw, instead of canvas.

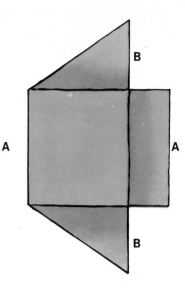

A different sort of two-pole tent   **1** Find two forked poles and hammer them firmly into the ground. Then join them with a third stake and tie them firmly together. Make the roof from a piece of canvas cut in the shape you see in fig. 2. Tie the canvas tightly to the crosswise pole at one end and fix the other end to the ground with pegs.

2 Before cutting the canvas, measure it carefully. A must be as wide as the distance between the stakes. B must be the length of the stakes.

A bamboo house   **1** Find four long bamboo canes, at least 1 cm. thick.

2 Bend them and fix them firmly into the ground at either end. Tie them together at the point where they all cross over.

3 Cover your house with a large, round piece of canvas, or lots of bits of material joined together with safety pins. You could use leafy branches too, straw, or even cardboard.

A wire-netting house   If you have a piece of wire-netting you almost have a house ready-made. Bend it to the shape you want and cover it with an old sheet, or whatever you can find.

A round wire-netting house   This is easy to make. Just bend the wire-netting into a cone and tie the two corners at the top. Leave the bottom open for a door. Careful! Wire-netting has lots of sharp bits sticking out.

Look at this amazing house. Is it the kind of house you would like to build? It has all sorts of hidden stairways, odd-shaped rooms and as you can see, there are already quite a few people living there.

Mr & Mrs Vinegar

Mr and Mrs Vinegar lived in a vinegar bottle. Mr Vinegar was long and thin and wore a string vest. Mrs Vinegar was short and fat and wore a frilly pink apron. The vinegar bottle was smelly but comfortable.

One day when Mr Vinegar was out visiting, Mrs Vinegar made up her mind to give their home a good spring cleaning. She took broom and brush and sponge and bucket and set to work singing. She worked hard, but she had bad luck. Her busy brush smacked against the side of the bottle, the glass cracked, and the whole house fell down, *tinkle tonkle*, on her head. Mrs Vinegar burst into tears. She ran to meet Mr Vinegar on his way home, and as soon as she saw him she called out:

"Oh, Mr Vinegar, Mr Vinegar, we are ruined, ruined, ruined!"

"Never mind ruin," said Mr Vinegar. He was an easygoing fellow and never made much fuss about anything.

But his wife went clucking up and down like a hen with nowhere to lay an egg, as was her way, until at last he asked, "Well, sweetie pie, how are we ruined?"

"Deary lordy mercy me," moaned Mrs Vinegar. "We are ruined because I've knocked the house down and it is all in little bits!"

"I see," said Mr Vinegar. "Well, never mind knocking the house down."

But Mrs Vinegar *did* mind, and she grew angry with her husband for being so calm about such a calamity. "You ought to feel something!" she screamed. And she hit him on the head with her rolling pin.

Mr Vinegar just smiled. He was used to this kind of thing. When she had finished hitting him on the head, he said, "There, sweetie pie, do you feel better now?"

"Yes," said Mrs Vinegar, drying her eyes with her apron. "I do."

"Good," said Mr Vinegar. "Now I suggest that there's no use in crying over a broken vinegar bottle. It's obvious what we must do."

"What's that?" asked Mrs Vinegar.

"Go back and get the door," said Mr Vinegar.

So they did. And when they had it, Mrs Vinegar said, "But what do we want the door for?"

"For our new house, of course," said Mr Vinegar. "All we have to do is find a house without a door, and then we fix our door on the hinge and go in and out and live there happily ever after. That's sensible, don't you think?"

Mrs Vinegar thought it was so sensible that she hit her husband on the head again with the rolling pin, just to celebrate the working of his brains. Then, with Mr Vinegar carrying the door on his back, they set out to see what they could see.

Five days later they came to a forest full of rhubarb trees. Mr Vinegar, bold in his string vest, did not hestitate. He plunged straight in. But Mrs Vinegar threw her pink apron over her head and began to shiver with anticipation.

"What's the matter, sweetie pie?" asked Mr Vinegar, who was beginning to find the door a burden.

"Anticipation," said Mrs Vinegar.

"What do you anticipate?" Mr Vinegar inquired politely.

"Custard," said Mrs Vinegar.

"Never mind custard," advised Mr Vinegar.

Mrs Vinegar gave her husband a black look. But she followed him and his advice into the rhubarb forest, where they barked their shins on a reasonable tree.

"My heart, my treasure, my little cabbage," said Mr Vinegar, "I will climb up into this reasonable tree, for the night is falling, and I will pull the door up after me, and then you too, and we can sleep on the door."

Mrs Vinegar was too tired to argue, so they did as Mr Vinegar suggested. Soon both Vinegars were curled snugly asleep on the door where it rested between the branches of the reasonable rhubarb tree. Mrs Vinegar dreamed of a husband who took things more seriously than Mr Vinegar. Mr Vinegar dreamed of a wife who kept her rolling pin for the pastry.

Just before dawn Mr Vinegar was awakened by the sound of voices from below.

"A guinea for you," said the first voice. "Two guineas for me."

"Rubbish," said the third voice, a very smooth and oily voice, like the voice of an educated but corrupt eel, "Gentlemen, let us not argue about such trivia. Kindly hand me the booty, Sebastian, and I shall divide it into fair dividends, after deducting my own expenses."

Mr Vinegar quickly awakened his wife by

tweaking her left ear. They peered down over the edge of the door and saw three robbers sitting under the tree. Two of the robbers carried huge knobbly clubs, and the third had a wicked-looking knife stuck in his leather belt. Mrs Vinegar began to shake.

"Why are you shaking?" whispered Mr Vinegar.

"Because they'll kill us if they find us," whispered his wife.

"Never mind killing," whispered Mr Vinegar.

This was too much. Mrs Vinegar was frightened, but she was so angry with her husband for saying never mind that she forgot her fright. She snatched the rolling pin from the pocket of her frilly apron and began hitting him over the head with it. She hit and hit.

"Sssh! Sssh!" hissed Mr Vinegar. "If you must hit me, do it quietly!"

"I will not!" screeched his wife. "Never mind killing indeed! Nitwit! Nincompoop! Take that, and that, and THAT!"

She screamed. The rolling pin thwacked. Mr Vinegar groaned.

To the robbers below, it all sounded like the noise of ghosts. They jumped up and ran around the tree trying to find somewhere to hide.

Mrs Vinegar gave her husband a final hefty whack. He toppled out of the tree. The door went with him. Door and husband fell on the robbers' heads!

Howling, yowling, the robbers ran away through the rhubarb forest.

Mr Vinegar sat up and rubbed his bruises. Then he looked to see if the door was all right. It had broken in half. Picking up the halves to see if he could fit them together again, Mr Vinegar saw dozens of golden guineas winking in the pale light of dawn.

"Golly," he said. And, "Come down, my darling," he called to his wife. "Come down from the reasonable tree and look at this! Our luck has changed! Our fortune's made!"

Mrs Vinegar came huffing down from the rhubarb tree. When she saw the money, she danced a jig for joy.

"Husband," she said, "you're not such a bad fellow."

"My jewel, my treasure, my little duck!" cried Mr Vinegar. "Thank you!"

Mrs Vinegar sat down quickly on a toadstool. She fanned her face with a fern.

"What are you doing, sweetie pie?" Mr Vinegar asked.

"Now that we are rich," explained Mrs Vinegar, "I can be a lady of leisure."

"What's leisure?" asked Mr Vinegar.

"Leisure," Mrs Vinegar said, "is sitting on toadstools and fanning yourself with ferns and never doing any cleaning or scrubbing."

"I see," said Mr Vinegar. "But what about my string vest?"

"Bother your string vest," said Mrs Vinegar.

Mr Vinegar thought about this. He did not like his string vest being bothered. But he thought he saw what his wife meant. "Oh, well," he said, "never mind."

47

Just imagine

The house on page 45 was strange, but you can invent some even odder and more wonderful houses yourself.

Think of all the things you like to play with. Perhaps they could be made into a house. Just imagine anything you would like. And if anyone tries to be practical and tell you that you can't make a house out of chocolate, or feathers, or a waterfall,

1 Laura painted an aquarium house, full of strange fish and plants so that anyone living there could imagine they were in a pool.

2 Loris invented a house in a shoe.

4 This is a toffee house, designed by Kate.

3 This is Joe's cloud house.

5 Martha likes to be warm, so her house is inside a cat.

don't worry. People are always doing the impossible. And anyway it's fun to think about really fantastic and strange things sometimes.

Would you like to live in a round house or perhaps in a cave underground? Or do you like any of the houses here? They were all painted by 10-year old children from different countries.

6 Lindy and Sue wanted to live on the moon, so they could see what Martians are really like.

7 Maria's house is made of ice cream and chocolate, so she can eat it if she gets hungry.

8 Sara's house is inside an elephant.

10 John's house is on a magic carpet.

9 Clare likes flowers, so she has made them into a house.

11 This is Danny's house in the sun, flying through the sky.

49

How a house is built

This picture shows how the artist, Jan Breughel the Elder, imagined the Tower of Babel. So the story goes, it was an amazing tower built long ago by some people who were trying to reach the sky. In those days, everyone spoke the same language and all the thousands of builders could understand and help one another. But God was angry because of their pride and he stopped them very simply — by making them all speak different languages. Straightaway, the builders started having all sorts of misunderstandings and the tower was never finished.

1 This is a small igloo, made by an eskimo when he needs a temporary shelter. He shapes blocks of ice and lays them in circles, one on top of another.

2 The blocks are welded together with snow, which quickly packs down into ice.

A house built of ice

It is easy to make a house to play in, but it is very difficult when you want to live in it all the time.

There are all sorts of things you need in a house. It must be big enough, for a start and then it has to protect you from the weather and maybe from thieves or some other kind of danger.

All over the world, people have built homes to suit their own particular needs. The Eskimos in the frozen North, for example, make large, dome-shaped houses out of ice in winter, because that is the best building material they have. In summer when it is warmer they live in tents made of animal skins. Everything inside an igloo is made of snow but it is still very warm and comfortable. Even the windows are made from a sheet of ice. In a family igloo, the door is usually at the end of a short tunnel so that the icy winds do not blow straight inside.

Nowadays many Eskimos no longer build in a traditional way. They live in houses made of concrete and depend on an air service to bring them all kinds of food and materials. In the same way, all over the world new materials and new designs are being worked out, often along side the more traditional ways of building. But it takes more than the planner to build a house. It needs the co-operation of lots of people, each with their own special job.

3 The art of building an igloo is making sure the last blocks fit exactly. To do this, an eskimo will get inside.

4 Eskimos sometimes make these little igloos when they are out hunting.

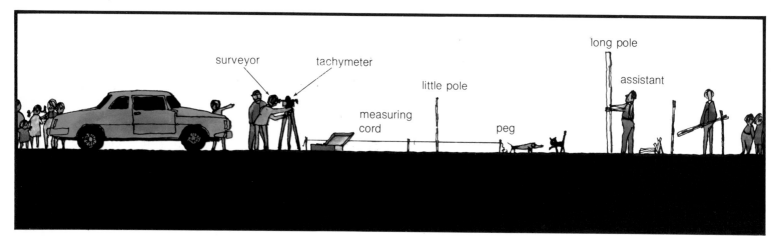

1 The Layout The layout is the plan of the house, laid out on the ground, exactly as it is to be built. Little pegs are stuck where the corners of the building will be, and they are joined together with string. The surveyor (he is the man looking through his tachymeter which is something that looks rather like a pair of binoculars on a stand) now checks all the measurements. He uses two red and white poles to help him judge the distances accurately. One is 3 m. high and is held by his assistant. The other one is smaller ($1\frac{1}{2}$ m. high) and is stuck in the ground between him and his assistant.

2 Digging the foundations When all the measurements of the layout are right, work begins on digging the foundations. This is the firm, flat base under the ground on which the house is solidly built. Once upon a time, workmen only had pickaxes and shovels; today, they can use an excavator. (You can see it in the picture.) This digs out the earth and tips it into a waiting truck. By now, the builders have set up a hut for the works manager (he is the man who sees that the work is done properly) and the site manager (he organizes *how* the work will be done). In the hut, they keep all the papers and plans that have to do with the building.

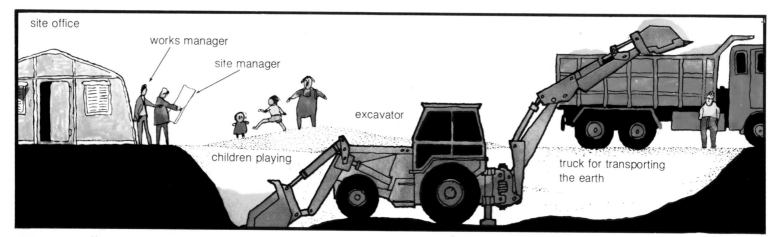

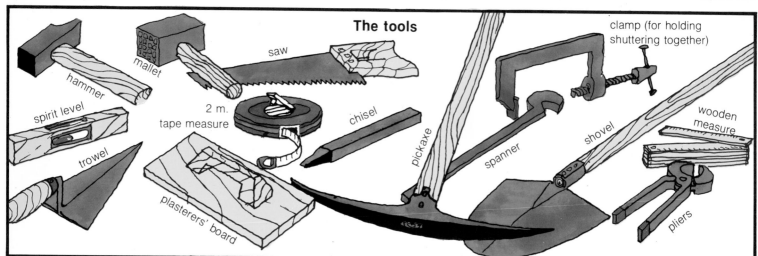

Buildings in our cities

Since ancient times, people have slowly developed methods of building. Sometimes these old ways are forgotten. For example, no one knows exactly how the ancient Egyptian pyramids were built. In most ways however, methods have improved and today in our towns and cities we build many of our houses in the same basic way. This does not mean that all houses are constructed in exactly the same fashion.

The next few pages show how builders might put up a block of flats in a city.

3   The foundations Work begins first of all, on the *structure*, which is the framework holding up the whole building. You can think of it as the skeleton of the building. This must be firmly rooted in the hole dug by the excavator. The structure is made of reinforced concrete, with the *piers* supporting the *beams* and *floors*. The piers are made like this: first, the builders make a hollow wooden box, open at one end. This is called the *shuttering*. They line it with a framework of steel rods and then wet concrete is poured in. When the concrete is hard, they take away the wooden shuttering. Each pier is firmly fixed in a *plinth*, or solid square foundation of its own.

4   The ground floor When the structure of the basement is finished, (which is where the cellars are) work begins on the ground floor. First of all, the builders put down a layer of large hollow bricks called *pots*. These bricks are made extra-strong with a framework of steel rods inside them. Then, this layer is completely covered with wet concrete. Floors can be made simply of solid reinforced concrete, but if pots are used, the floors are much lighter, and also much less expensive.

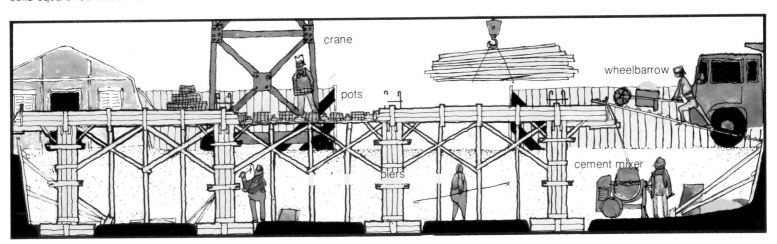

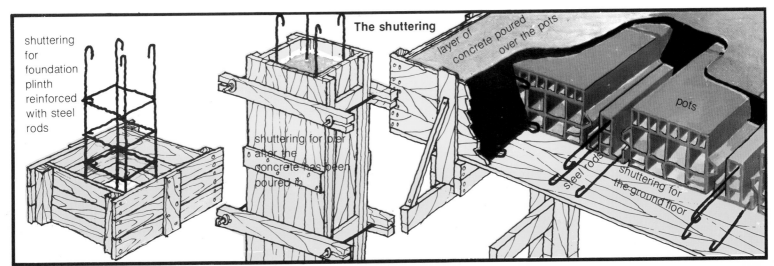

little tree

shaft for lift
and stair well

builders celebrating

crane

scaffolding

pier

ground floor

plinth

5 Finishing the structure Floor after floor goes up until the structure is complete. Now it is made up of foundation *plinths*, reinforced concrete *piers* joined by *beams* of reinforced concrete, or sometimes steel. Each floor is made of either *reinforced concrete*, or *pots*. Of course, there is also the scaffolding, which the builders need to stand on and work.

When the last floor is complete, everyone has a party. In some countries, they put a small branch or tree on top so that everyone knows the building has stopped growing.

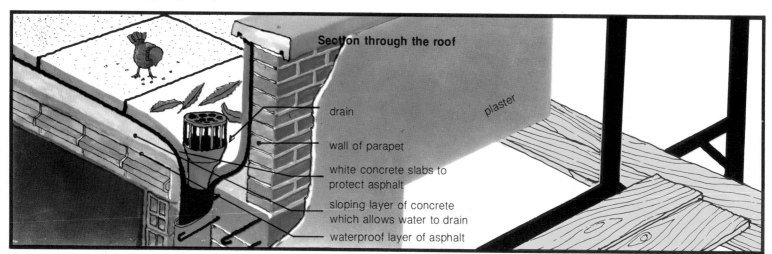

Section through the roof

plaster

drain

wall of parapet

white concrete slabs to
protect asphalt

sloping layer of concrete
which allows water to drain

waterproof layer of asphalt

brick work

NOOR

window

children watching

plaster

6 The rough shell and the smooth finish Once the structure is finished, then every bit of wood is taken from the concrete beams, piers and floors. Now the brick walls can be built and the door and window frames put in. Once all this basic building has been done, we have what we call the rough shell. Work can begin on making everything smooth and finished.

Plaster is spread on the walls with a special trowel and the floors are given a special layer of concrete to make them level. Now tiles can be laid in the bathroom or kitchen. Have you noticed how builders put a squiggle of white paint on the windows of a new, empty building? That is to warn people that glass is there.

Structure of the walls

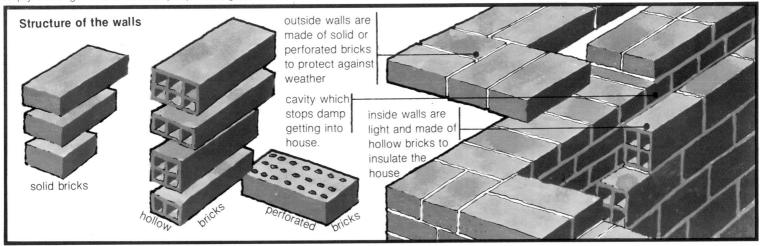

solid bricks

hollow bricks

perforated bricks

outside walls are made of solid or perforated bricks to protect against weather

cavity which stops damp getting into house.

inside walls are light and made of hollow bricks to insulate the house

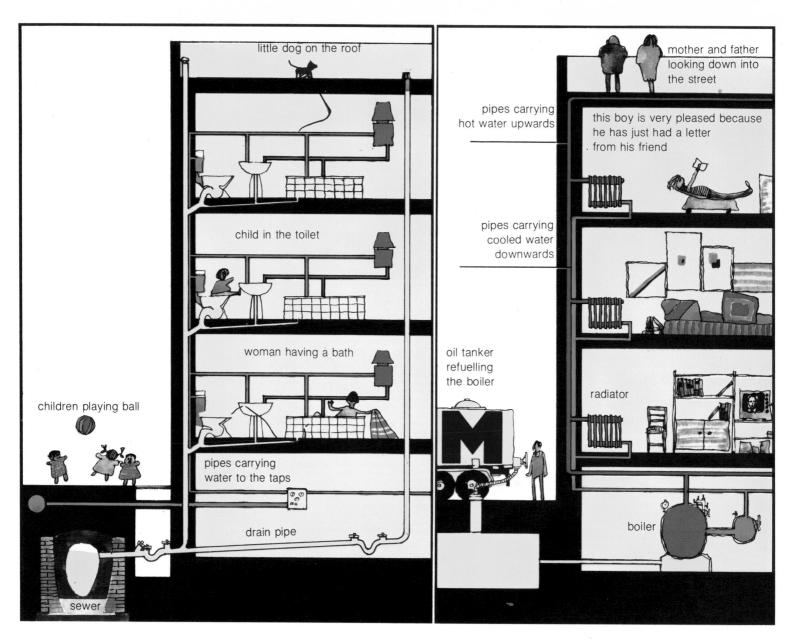

little dog on the roof

mother and father looking down into the street

pipes carrying hot water upwards

this boy is very pleased because he has just had a letter from his friend

child in the toilet

pipes carrying cooled water downwards

oil tanker refuelling the boiler

woman having a bath

radiator

children playing ball

pipes carrying water to the taps

drain pipe

boiler

sewer

7 The water system This is put in as soon as the basic work has been finished. You can see how it works from the picture.

In the blue pipes, cold water is going to the taps and water heaters. The water in our taps is under pressure. That means that it is being pushed along. Otherwise, of course, it would not go uphill to our taps. The water in the red pipes has been heated in a water heater The water in the yellow pipes is dirty, and flows down into the drain.

Can you see a dark grey house in the middle of the brown ones? Do you like it? If you don't, invent a different house to fit there.

8 The heating system There are many different ways of heating a house. How many can you think of? — coal, gas, electricity — and there are several more. But large buildings are usually heated by a big boiler.

This heats the water which is then carried (in the red pipes) to all the rooms. When the water cools down, it flows back (in the blue pipes) to the boiler, where it is heated up again. A boiler can run on any kind of fuel, but more often it uses oil or gas.

little girl waiting for her father

children playing with a dog

gas pipes

meter

cat looking for mice

girl using a hair drier

this man is having a rest

cable covered with plastic carrying electric current

lady cleaning the house with a vacuum cleaner

electric fire

electric light

meter.

9 The gas system In the country, if people want to have gas in their homes, they often have to buy huge cans full of gas, called *cylinders*. But in a town, gas can be sent to the houses in a pipe. You can often see workmen in the street laying a gas pipe to a house. In this picture, the gas pipes are in blue. They are carrying the gas into the house. There is also a meter in every house which measures the gas we use, and also one for the electricity.

10 Electricity We use electricity to light our homes, for our freezers, televisions, telephones and sometimes for our cookers and heaters. What things in your house run on electricity? Do you know how it reaches your house? Well, in most cases, it comes in a thick cable or wire, covered with plastic and buried safely in the wall, so that it won't give anyone an electric shock. It is in red in this picture. Electricity, like gas, can be very dangerous if it is not controlled carefully.

1 This is a bow window from a house in London.

2 This window, with its curtain of chains, belongs to a temple in Tibet.

3 A perfectly ordinary window in Italy. But it does have three beautiful blue umbrellas in it!

4 This beautifully decorated window is typical of some of the old houses in Lebanon.

Windows, doors and balconies

Houses are big, small, exciting, dull; beautiful and ugly — but they do have some things in common.

If you want sunlight in your house, you need windows. If you want to be able to get in and out easily, there must be a door (unless you want to be always jumping out of the windows). And if you want to be outside, without having to go actually

9 This balcony overlooks the bazaar in Fez, Morocco.

10 This patio belongs to a house in India.

13 The door of a judge's house in Meimand, a village cut out of rock, in Iran.

15 A hut in Goa, Southern India.

◁**14** The door of a Polish railway station, beautifully decorated with traditional designs.

5 This window is in Nepal and it is a very interesting shape.

6 Pigeons live in this window, which is made of boxes. It is in Turkey.

7 This window in Buenos Aires is made of stained glass.

8 This window with its hearts and flowers is in California.

outside your house, you need to have balconies.

But these basic things can come in many thousands of different shapes and sizes, as you can see here. They can also be used in many ways, for example, in hot countries, the windows are often carefully placed to keep the air circulating — the earliest form of air conditioning.

11 These are balconies in a hotel in San Francisco, California.

12 Patios and balconies in the old quarter of Seville, Spain.

17 Door of a hut in Thoda.

18 A chicken house in England. There seems to be a very strange chicken living there.

◁**16** Door of a mausoleum in Kashan, Iran.

Roofs, stairs and courtyards

1 Stone steps in a house in Viterbo, Italy.

A house needs a roof. Without a roof a building may look pretty, but it's not much good as a home. That's why people say sometimes, "I want a roof over my head," meaning, "I want to have somewhere I can live." In hot, dry countries, people use their flat roofs for drying grain and also for sleeping on. In cooler, wetter lands the roofs are sloping so that rain or snow can run off.

Roofs can be made of all kinds of material depending on where the people are living. For example, a thatched roof is made from bundles of straw or reeds which help to keep the cottage warm in winter and cool in summer. In Japan where there are often earthquakes, people make roofs of wood because they are easier to rebuild and of course, not so dangerous if they fall. In many countries, important buildings were roofed with lead, bronze, or even copper so that they should last longer. But of course this is very expensive.

2 These steps outside an old Swiss house are covered with ivy and flowers.

3 Stairs in a house in Barcelona, Spain, designed by a famous architect called Gaudí.

4 Can you see the cat? He belongs to a Czechoslovakian farm worker.

5 This is a very old spiral stairway in Venice, Italy.

6 Fire escapes in an old tenement block, New York.

7 This secret courtyard is in Sciacca, in Sicily.

8 This courtyard with a roof is in Egypt.

9 Courtyards in two old houses in Gafsa, Tunisia.

10 The wooden roof of a monastery in Shofakuji, Japan.

11 This decorated roof is part of a Turk's house.

12 These up-and-down roofs belong to a Buddhist temple in Bangkok.

13 Old roofs in Prague. They have steep slopes so that the snow can slip off them.

15 Pretty brown-speckled roofs in Venice, Italy.

Today, most modern buildings have roofs of tiles or reinforced concrete.

We tend to take stairs for granted. After all, everyone says 'upstairs' and 'downstairs'. But they too are very important if your house has more than one floor. It would be annoying to have lots of rooms you couldn't reach!

Not every house has a courtyard, but you will see them in most older towns and cities. A courtyard is a piece of land completely surrounded by a building. Often it is like a walled garden.

Many years ago, big houses would nearly always have very fine large courtyards. That is where guests would be received. And as important people tended to travel with a large group of servants, they needed a lot of space.

14 Dome-like roofs in Iran. They are open at the sides so that the air can circulate easily.

16 In Polignano in Apulia, Italy, the roofs form little terraces to collect the rain water.

17 A magnificent courtyard in the Palace of Beit Edine in the Lebanon.

18 This is a triangular courtyard in the church of Beit Mariam in Ethiopia.

19 A quiet courtyard in a village on the Island of Rhodes, Greece.

A skyscraper **1** Find a piece of paper marked with squares and fold it in two.

2 Then fold it in four by bringing the outer edges into the middle.

3 Next, unfold the piece of paper, and following the squares, draw lots of little windows.

4 Fold the piece of paper again so it is hollow in the middle, and join the two sides with sticky tape. Now you have a skyscraper.

Model houses

If you like thinking up play-houses indoors, you might like to make some model houses as well. Maybe you already know about them, but there should be something here to give you some new ideas. Because these are just the beginning: it is up to you to be as simple or as complicated and fantastic as you like. You will get better results if you use stiff paper and it is a good idea to include all kinds of different models with your houses; for example, cars, animals, trees and people. Why not put things inside your houses, so that it looks as if they are living there? If you liked, you could also make a street full of houses, with a factory, skyscrapers and even a garage.

A factory **1** Find a piece of polystyrene (it is often used for packing). Cut out a bit which looks like the kind of factory you want. Ask an adult for help when using polystyrene.

2 Draw in the windows with a felt-tip pen.

3 Make pipes out of straws and fasten with pins.

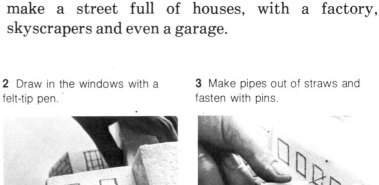

4 To make a chimney, cut a piece of card into a rectangle.

5 Roll it into a tube and join the sides with sticky tape.

6 Here is a finished factory. What does yours look like?

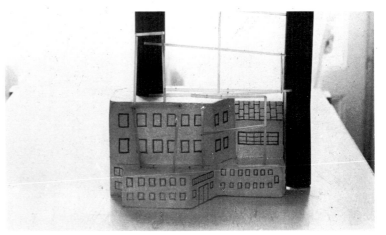

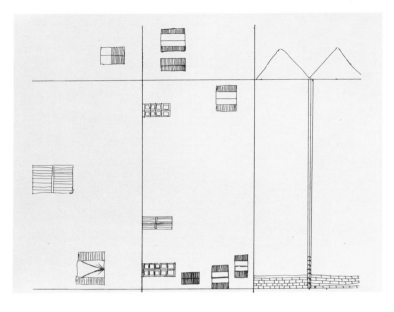

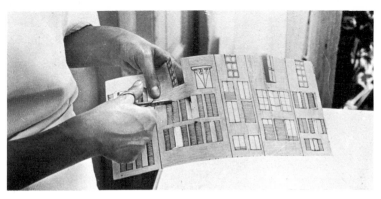

A paper house **1** Fold a piece of paper into three equal parts. On two of them, draw the walls of the house (remember to put two walls on each strip) and on the third, draw the roof. You can colour them if you like. Cut the paper into three along the folds. Now, if you cut the doors and windows out on three sides only, you will be able to make them open and shut.

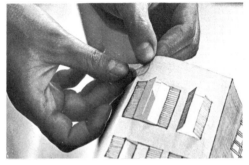

2 Fold your two strips of walls to make the corners of the house, as you see here.

3 Join the two strips with sticky tape so that the house now has four sides.

4 Cut out the roof, fold it as you see here and join it at either end with sticky tape.

5 Now stand the four walls of your house on a piece of white paper and draw round them with a felt-tip pen.

6 Next, draw in a garden on the white paper. Do you want a garden path?

7 You could also make a fence or a wall with a strip of paper, but remember to measure it first.

8 Finally, put the roof on the walls, fix the house in the garden and add anything else you like; flowers, trees, or maybe some animals.

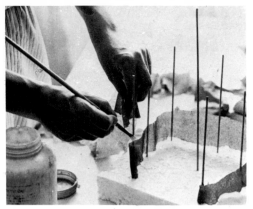

A hut **1** Stick eight little sticks in a circle on a thick piece of polystyrene. Put a longer one in the middle.

2 Glue pieces of thin paper all around the circle of sticks, starting from the bottom, until you have completely covered your hut.

3 Try not to put on too much glue and use different colours and lengths of paper. This makes your hut look even better.

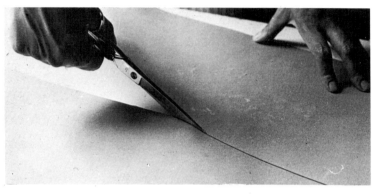

A round house **1** Cut out a large rectangular strip of card.

2 Draw windows and doors on this strip and then cut them out on three sides only, so that they will open and shut.

3 Now roll the card into a tube and join the two sides together with sticky tape.

4 Next, find a plate slightly larger than the width of the house. Put it on a piece of corrugated cardboard and draw round it. This is going to be the roof.

5 Cut it out, and put it on top of your house, fixing it on with sticky tape.

6 You can make a wall round your house with a thin strip of card joined with sticky tape.

7 You can make bigger houses by balancing your first house on top of another two smaller ones. Why not make a garden too, with twigs and leaves stuck on with sticky tape?

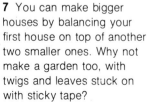

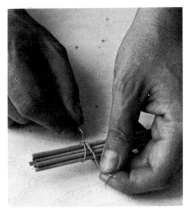
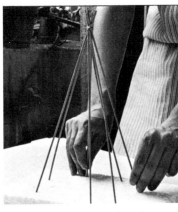

An Indian tepee   1 Tie together at one end, eight little sticks of the same length.

2 Open them out at the other end and stick them into a piece of polystyrene.

3 Cut up some strips of material or thin paper and glue them around the sticks, from the bottom upwards.

4 Leave a hole for the door. Now here is the finished tepee. And here are some Indians, too.

A corrugated cardboard house   1 Corrugated cardboard is a special kind of packing paper made with little crinkles. Cut out a long strip.

2 Completely cut out the windows.

3 Stick the pieces you have cut out underneath the holes, to make big window ledges.

4 Join the two ends of your house with sticky tape.

5 Make the house in the shape you want with sticky tape.

6 Put your house on another bit of cardboard and draw round it.

7 Cut out the shape and glue it on top of your walls. Now you have a roof.

8 Little squares of grease-proof paper make good glass for your windows.

9 You can make chimneys with little rolls of card.

10 Your house is finished; but of course there is always room for new ideas. Why not build a skylight? Or maybe a garage?

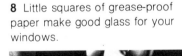

A bit of bad luck

How a village is built

1 This is a large photograph of the same group of houses as you can see on the facing page. They are all part of a deserted *Pueblo* village made by North American Indians, many, many years ago. We don't know why they had to leave. Perhaps they were attacked by enemies or perhaps it was because the weather became very much hotter and drier.

2 An old deserted village built by the Pueblo Indians in the Mesa Verde, Colorado, USA.

A village in a mountain

Up until now, we have only been talking about houses. But houses nearly always come in groups because on the whole people prefer to live together. For one thing, it is much easier to organize shops, lighting, heating, postal services and many other such things that most of us find necessary for everyday life. Even in olden times, people tended to live in groups because this meant they were safe from attack by wild beasts or robbers. It was also easier for them to hunt or fish or farm. It's exciting to see the hero in a film fighting a grizzly bear on his own; but not everyone can manage it. Certainly not all the time, anyway.

Therefore when they were choosing a place to build their village, people would think of two main things. First, where could they find some way of getting food and water? And second, where would they be safe? For example, the fishing villages in Sardinia are built on the coast — but they can hardly ever be seen from the sea. This is because the fishermen wanted to be safe from pirates.

But villagers thought not only about places where they would be safe, but also about places they could defend. They would build on top of a hill, or in a narrow gap in the mountains or as you have seen, in caves underground. They might even live on the banks of a fast-flowing river or in the middle of a lake.

Look how safe the *Pueblo* village is. There would probably have been only one or two secret entrances — unless you had a helicopter! The Indians who lived here grew vegetables and wove the most beautiful baskets. They were not warlike, but they still had to make sure they were not attacked. Among the living-houses, there is a special round house called a *kiva*, or magic house, where the medicine-man prepared for important ceremonies. The Indians believed that everything had a spirit and that man, the sky and the earth, were all bound up with each other. This is why they would have special magic dances to bring rain, to make the corn grow or to ask the spring sun to return. It was a way of showing that as man is part of nature, he should live in harmony with all living things.

A village on the edge of a cliff

Look at this little village. It looks a bit like a bunch of houses on an open hand. In fact, it is called Pentedattilo, which in the local language means "five fingers". A long time ago, a castle was built here commanding the valley. It was a good place to choose because no one was likely to attack from the top of the mountain. And of course, anyone coming up from the valley would not have an easy time either.

The village of Pentedattilo grew up around the castle. Like the *Pueblo* Indians, the villagers felt they were safe from their enemies on such a steep hillside. Their houses are tightly packed together just like the *Pueblo* Indian village too. This is partly to be safer, and also, because there isn't much space to build on! Today, they still grow their olives and grapes as they have done for hundreds of years, but the castle has long since disappeared.

This village in Italy is called Pentedattilo. It was built on a steep hillside so that it would be easy to defend.

A village on stilts—on land

This pretty village is in the far-away Celebes Islands, in Indonesia. The people who live here are called the Toradja, which means, "people of the mountains", and they build their houses on stilts. Many people build this way in tropical countries because houses are safer off the ground. It also means that when it is very hot, they can catch every breeze and when it rains a great deal their houses do not get water-logged and rotten so quickly. But why do these houses look like boats?

Old Toradja legends say that many, many years ago, long before anyone now living was born, the Toradja people arrived by sea in boats and went to live in the mountains. Perhaps that is why they built their new houses to look like boats, too.

1 This is a Toradja village in the Celebes. The houses look like boats.

2 Toradja houses are all decorated with beautiful coloured patterns and wooden carvings.

3 This shows the inside of one of the houses. This Toradja grandmother is making the bed.

1 This is one of the San Blas Islands in the Antilles. At four years old, children know how to swim and by the time they are eight, they can fish with a harpoon.

A village in a lagoon

In the Antilles, off Central America, there are some tiny islands called San Blas. They are in a huge lagoon, sheltered by coral reefs. You can see how the island in the picture above is covered with houses. If it was in the open sea, they would soon be swept away by storms.

The Cuna Indians who live here grow coconuts on the other islands in the lagoon. There are plenty of trees and plenty of nuts for everyone. The day-to-day life of the village is organized mainly by the women and the men help mostly with the heavy work. The people here seem very happy and don't want to change their way of life at all. Do you think it sounds a good way to live?

2 This is one of the islands where the San Blas Indians look after the coconut palms. Coconuts are very good to eat and you can also get tough fibres and oil from them.

1 These houses on the edge of the forest are part of the village of Zdiar, Czechoslovakia.

A village on the edge of the forest

2 The doors and windows open inwards because of the snow.

Now we are in the mountains of Czechoslovakia. This group of houses belongs to one family. These farmers and woodmen live on the edge of the forest.

As you can see from the picture there is only one door to their houses, which they keep very firmly shut when wolves are about. See how steep the roofs are. This is so that the snow can slip off easily in winter.

3 There is only one door and it is tightly barred when there are wolves about.

1 This is a hut in the Crahò village. Can you see a mother and her two children, a little boy and girl?

A round village

People have always thought that circles are rather special. In legends and fairytales, magicians and witches make magic circles that no one can enter and everyone has heard stories of magic rings with wonderful powers. Why? Maybe it is something to do with the fact that a circle is unbroken. You can go round and round for ever without coming to the end.

Perhaps that is why these people have chosen to build their villages in the shape of a circle. A more practical reason is that a circle is much easier to defend than any other shape. Can you see why?

Here are some pictures of the Crahò Indians who live in the Amazon jungle, which is perhaps the largest and wildest in the world. These Indians believe that inside the circle, which they call a *kraal*, they are safe from all the evil things in the jungle and at night, they bring all their animals there. Paths lead from their houses to the centre of the circle, like spokes in a wheel, and right in the middle they have their meeting place, where the whole village gathers to talk and dance and eat together.

2 This is inside one of the huts. The Crahò Indians sleep in hammocks and sometimes even on the table.

3 This strange round village is in the huge forests of the Amazon in South America.

A fortified village

You must know what an onion looks like. It is made up of lots of skins. You can peel them off, one after the other until you get to the middle. This village was built rather like an onion. It is one of the many fortified villages in the valley of the Drà in Morocco.

The villagers wanted to protect themselves from desert bandits, so they built walls and towers around their homes. But as they had hardly any stone or wood to use as building material, they had to use sun-baked mud and straw. Time passed, winter and summer, and the walls began to crumble. So the people decided to build another set of defences around the old walls to make them strong again. Maybe the village had become larger too, and they needed more room. This happened many times until the village looked as it does today.

Inside the walls, the houses are built around a square, where the people meet. They also keep their animals safe there at night. The Arabs who live there are mostly farmers and herdsmen and a village like this is called a *ksar*.

1 These mothers and children are coming home to their village in the evening. Can you see the bundles on their heads? ▶

2 This looks like an enormous castle, but it is a fortified village in the valley of the River Drà, in Morocco.

A village dug out of rock

Thousands of years ago, many people lived in caves, because they were such good shelter from wind, sun and rain. They chose caves near a river so that they had water to drink (washing was not thought so important!), and they also liked to be near the sea, because then they could have fresh fish and shellfish to eat. Since those times there have always been people living either in natural caves or ones they have dug out for themselves. In the dry, hilly areas of the Canary Islands, near Africa, there are still people living in volcanic caves. They make ready-made homes in a place where there is little other building material.

This village is part of a town called Guadix, in Spain. It has been almost entirely dug out of the rocks. The first people who lived here left long ago and today the villagers are some gipsies, who have given up wandering for a settled life.

1 This village is part of a town called Guadix in Spain. It has been dug out of the rocks.

2 The houses are inside the rock and all you can see from the outside is a door, a window and the chimney.

3 The chimneys have two uses. They let smoke out and they also let in air, when the front door is shut.

76

A village made to measure

This African village belongs to one of the Dogon tribes in Mali, Africa. Each of the houses, whether it is stone or mud, has something special about it. It has been built to fit one particular family. The villagers literally build their houses around themselves, putting in doors, windows and walls exactly as they need them.

Once the house is built, the family divides it up — a room for grandmother and grandfather, a room for the children, a room for the parents, a kitchen, and so on. In front of each house is a granary where the family keeps their millet; for everyone here does a little farming. (Millet is a kind of grain.) The men work in the fields while the women keep house and look for extra sorts of food and fuel. Even the children do their share of work.

This is a Dogon village in Mali, Africa. Here, everyone builds their own house exactly as they need it.

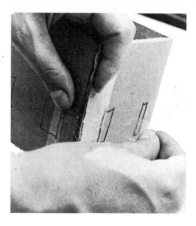

A fortified village   1 Cut strips of corrugated cardboard, draw doors and windows and then fold them in four. Now join the two edges and cover with a roof.

2 Use the handle of a pair of scissors to make the folds.

3 Make all your joins with sticky tape.

A model village

Making a village can be even more interesting than building a house on its own. In your village you can put streets, squares, gardens — maybe even a river or a lake. Then you can fill it with people and animals and make up lots of adventures for them. You could have parties, dances, battles and ambushes — anything you can think of.

You might like to try out some of these ideas for making a village. But remember; if you want, you can work out more complicated plans for yourself. Why not make some of the villages in the pictures in this book? Or perhaps even a village you have seen in real life. You can use any of the houses, castles, tents and huts you saw on pages 30 and 62.

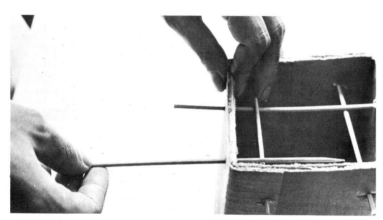

A Dogon village   1 Make some houses just as you did for the fortified village, but don't put on a roof. Then thread four little sticks through the walls of each house, as you can see here.

2 Cut out a roof just a little smaller than the house and balance it on the sticks.

3 Spread some little strips of paper on the roof to look like straw drying in the sun.

4 To make straw roofs, fold a piece of paper in half, then fold it in half again *the same way*. Cut it into little strips almost to the end. Now roll it into the shape you see here and fix with sticky tape.

5 Your finished village might look a bit like this. If you want to make cone-shaped roofs, look at page 31. The palm tree is a straw roof stuck the other way up into a long, thin cylinder of corrugated cardboard.

 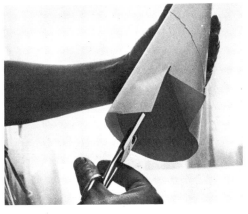 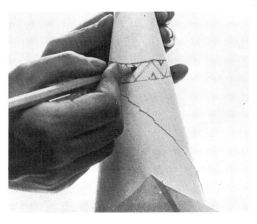

An American Indian village **1** Make some paper cones with a hole at the top.

2 Cut out and fold back an opening in the tent, as you see here.

3 Draw any pattern you like on the tents.

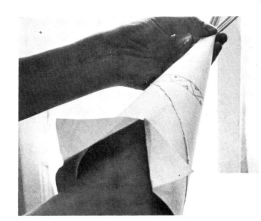 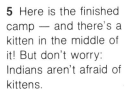 

4 Put some straws through the holes at the top, and fix them with sticky tape.

5 Here is the finished camp — and there's a kitten in the middle of it! But don't worry: Indians aren't afraid of kittens.

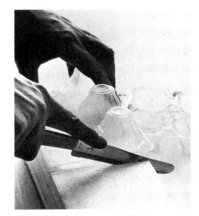 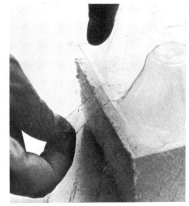  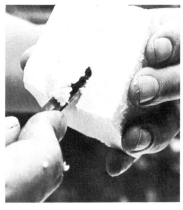

A domed village **1** Find a piece of polystyrene about the same size as an egg box.

2 Fix the top of the egg box to the polystyrene and you have a house with six domes.

3 If you want smaller houses, cut the individual pockets out of the egg box.

4 Then carefully cut little squares of polystyrene, the same size as the pockets. Cut out the door with a pen knife.

A polystyrene village You can make a really amazing village out of different shapes of polystyrene glued together. Draw on doors and windows, too, if you like.

5 With enough egg boxes, you can build a whole city — but someone will have to eat lots of eggs!

1 This is a Kafir village in the Himalayas, the highest mountains in the world.

Life in a village

This village is in a region of Eastern Afghanistan, in the Himalayas. It lies in the Bumburet valley and the people who live here are Kafirs. (They are nothing to do with the Kaffirs who live in Africa). A long time ago, the followers of the Prophet Mohammed began fighting all the countries they could in order to convert them to the religion of Islam. But for many years the Kafirs would not be persuaded, because they are extremely independent and their fortified mountain villages were difficult to attack. In fact the word *Kafir* comes from the Arabic for "infidel" or "unbeliever". Finally however, they were forced to give in and the country is now known as Nuristan, or "the land of the enlightened".

The Kafirs are something of a mystery because they are fair-skinned and some people believe that as a race they are related much more closely to the West than the East. They are very proud people; but because life in these mountains is very hard, they have to work together to grow food and all important decisions are made at the village council. Women are treated with great respect here, and everyone plays their part in everyday life. There is little flat land and so their fields are very small, but

2 This is the village seen from above. The Kafirs use their roofs for drying grain.

◁ 3 Here is a Kafir house, built like a small fort.

4 Inside a house. Can you see the beautifully patterned carpet on the floor?

5 The Kafirs put statues like these on their tombs.

nearly everyone keeps a few goats or cattle as well as growing wheat, corn and vegetables. Most Kafirs don't know how to read or write, and so they teach each other everything they know by singing, dancing and reciting. That is how many of our legends and fairytales began; by people handing down stories by word of mouth.

This is just an ordinary village; but it does show some special things about village life, which are true for many villages all over the world. When life is hard, the villagers must work together, make their important decisions together and of course, they usually all know one another. Originally, all villagers were farmers and craftsmen, growing or making everything they needed for themselves. Today that is no longer true everywhere and you probably know a village yourself, where the people are not self-supporting. But it is still true that life is much calmer than in the city and villagers often have a routine that changes only with the seasons. Do you think this is the best way to live — or can you think of any disadvantages? If you can, do you still think it would be more pleasant to live in a village than in a city?

6 The Kafirs make delicious cakes for a festival.

7 Kafir women dancing at the Spring festival. It's a time when everyone can really let themselves go. ▷

The beginnings of a city

How cities grew up

Villages are usually small and cities are big. You might think that villages are baby towns; but this is not quite true. Cities are different; not only in size, but because the people who live there do different things.

Look at this picture of an old city. It is in a very barren place and there is nowhere to grow any food. So why are people living there? If you look carefully, you can see waggons arriving by land and there is also a good harbour for boats. These people are living by trade.

Trade began when people started swopping the goods they grew or made for other things they needed. A farmer would give his friend some chickens and a bag of corn for a beautifully embroidered coat, or perhaps a carpet. This is called *barter*. As you can imagine, there was plenty of room for argument and people might discuss for many hours how much each thing was worth. In some countries today, they still do not have fixed prices and you can arrange with the shopkeeper how much he is going to charge you.

After a while people began using money, because it was easier to carry. It was also easier to have something that was worth a fixed amount. They began travelling many miles to sell or barter and so they needed a place where everyone could meet. This is how markets began. Can you see the market in the picture? It is full of little stalls where people are selling food, clothes, jewelry and furniture. There is a lot of choice for anyone who has enough money. Markets also had to be somewhere that lots of people could reach easily. Cities were in places like this; for example on the coast, or where two big roads meet.

Cities depend very much on people coming into them to bring food and good things. They could not manage without outside help. They also needed to be defended as you can see from the towers in the picture. Perhaps these people were afraid of pirates!

1 Here are the walls of the ancient deserted city of Bam in Iran. It looks rather like a beautiful sandcastle.

2 This is a square in the centre of Bam. Do you see the fortifications? This is where the people fought off enemy attacks.

Cities from long ago: Bam in Iran

What did cities look like, many hundreds of years ago? Today, even our oldest cities have been changed over the years and it is hard to say exactly how they were originally. Perhaps the best way to see is to have a look at some different deserted cities, where the people left long ago never to return. Of course these cities are now in ruins, but they have not been built over and so you can see clearly how the houses were laid out.

Here you can see Bam, in Iran, abandoned so long ago that we don't really know the reason why. Perhaps it was because the water dried up in the nearby rivers; or maybe it was because the important merchants and traders took their goods along another route and stopped coming here.

From here, it looks as if it has been made out of sand, although it was actually built from sun-baked mud and straw.

3 Another view of Bam, with its ruined roads and houses.

1 This is Fatehpur-Sikri, a deserted city in India. Inside this palace, the emperor would receive any of his subjects who wanted to speak with him.

2 The emperor's throne used to be next to this pillar, inside the palace.

Cities from long ago: Fatehpur-Sikri in India

Fatehpur-Sikri is rather a special city, because its people only lived there for a very short while and it has been almost perfectly preserved. It was built on a red sandstone ridge, not far from Agra, where, according to legend, there once lived a holy man called Shaikh Salim.

At that time in Northern India, there was a great Mohgul emperor called Akbar. Akbar was very unhappy because all his sons had died at birth. He asked Shaikh for help and the holy man blessed him.

Some time later, the queen had a fine son and Akbar was so grateful that he built a magnificent city on the spot where the holy man lived. Its walls were seven miles long and the emperor and his family lived here in great state.

Sadly, fifteen years later, there was a terrible drought and this is why everyone had to leave the city. They never returned. The emperor's son, Jahangir, however, grew up and ruled the empire after his father's death.

3 This is the emperor's Summer Palace. Under the bridge was an artificial pool but it has since dried up.

1 This is the main square of the deserted jungle city of Tikal. This is where the Mayas had all kinds of important festivals and meetings.

Cities from long ago: Tikal in Guatemala

Deep in the jungle of Guatemala, there is one of the most mysterious deserted cities in the world. It is also perhaps one of the most beautiful. It belonged to a great people called the Mayas, who had an enormous empire many, many years ago. Today, only the great, pyramid-shaped temples, the palace, the squares and the market remain.

It seems that the lords and priests lived inside the city, while the poorer Indians stayed outside, growing fruit and vegetables. It wasn't a city as we think of one today, because very few people actually lived there. It was a place for all kinds of important ceremonies. Why did the Mayas go? We aren't really sure, except that we know they ruled the local Indians very strictly. Perhaps they rose up against their Maya overlords and drove them out. Certainly, there are still a few Indians living outside the city in straw huts to this day.

2 A group of pyramid-shaped temples in Tikal, Guatemala.

3 The Indians' huts in the jungle surrounding Tikal.

This is a cartoon drawing of what Tikal might have looked like once. Can you see the builders at work, carving the stone? Perhaps some of the buildings were used for looking at the stars, because we know that the Mayas were very clever astronomers. They worked out a very complicated calendar, even though they didn't know that the earth goes round the sun. They also worked out a set of hieroglyphics (picture writing) which is very pretty to look at, although we don't really understand what it means today. In the front of the picture, the local Indians are bringing food to the Maya priests.

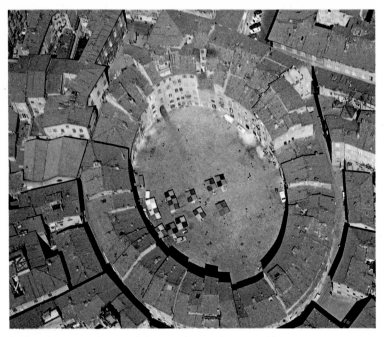

1 This square in Lucca, Italy, was an ancient *amphitheatre,* where the Romans held all kinds of open air shows. Over the years, people built on it and used the space in the middle for a market.

2 In medieval times, towns were often fighting each other, so they had to have strong walls and towers to defend themselves. In San Gimignano, Italy, the square (which is, in fact, triangle-shaped!) is completely surrounded by towers.

Eight Italian cities and their squares

Old cities often grew up around a central point. Sometimes it was a castle, a cathedral or a palace. Most often, especially in European countries, it was a square where people met for festivals, fairs, markets and public announcements. All the squares on these two pages come from Italy, which is famous for its beautiful squares.

Although there are often lots of little squares too, the main square is usually the heart of the city.

Houses are built around it and you can see how these old cities began growing from their central square. Even the roads led out from it, so that people could get in and out of the city easily. But that was before our modern traffic. Today, we try not to build our motorways through the middle of a city; instead, we often build a ring road round the outside. This is because instead of giving the city a shape, a motorway tends to split it up into traffic

3 This is one of the most beautifully designed squares in Italy. It is the Piazza della Santissima Annunziata in Florence. *Piazza* is the Italian word for *square.*

4 The Great Square in Vigevano, Italy, has the cathedral at one end. The arcades, all exactly alike, make it look a bit like a huge, open hall.

5 In Ferrara, Italy, there is a whole area of fine streets and squares built at a time we now call the *Renaissance*, when Italian architects, painters and musicians made some of the most beautiful art the world has ever seen. The square you can see is the Piazza Ariostea.

6 Grammichele was completely re-built after it had been flattened by an earthquake. The city takes its shape from the six-sided central square and six main roads leave from this point.

islands. No one wants to have to cross an eight-lane highway to reach the shops!

Grammichele (fig. 6) is an example of a city which has been designed round a central square. This sort of city grows up most often when it has been built and planned in a short space of time. Some of our modern cities have been built to a plan — can you think of any? On the other hand, cities which have been growing over hundreds of years often have lots of centres and are not at all regular in shape. Many

cities today also have suburbs, which blur their original plan. These really make another city outside the city. The people here want to work in the centre, but they prefer to have their homes outside.

One of the things you notice most about a city is that there are lots and lots of people. This doesn't mean that they all know each other. After all, it's not possible to make thousands of friends. In fact, some people say that cities are quite lonely places. Do you agree?

7 The Piazza in Borgo di Venaria Reale is made up of two beautiful curved palaces with arcades.

8 The little main square of Capri is surrounded by a jumble of old houses, churches and narrow streets. It is a favourite spot for both locals and tourists.

1 This is Nördlingen, a small town in Germany. It was built at a time when towns often fought amongst themselves and so it is surrounded by strong walls.

Cities all over the world

Do you remember the circular village in the Amazon (page 74)? Cities were also often built roughly in a circle, because that is the best shape for defence. You can see why, by looking at the picture of Nördlingen (fig. 1). In those days, cities were often at war with one another. When times became more peaceful, buildings began to sprawl out into the countryside.

About a hundred and fifty years ago, the Emperor Napoleon decided that Paris ought to be a modern city. He wanted it to have space, light, and a regular shape. He found architects who began to knock down the old medieval centre of the city and rebuild it as it is today. Many American cities were originally built to a very regular shape, but as they got bigger, they spread out in all directions.

2 Here is another fortified town, this time in Italy. It is called Palmanova. The rulers of Venice built it long ago to keep out the Turks and Austrians. The high walls have been made in the shape of a star with nine points. Six roads lead out from the six-sided main square.

3 Bangkok is the capital of Thailand. It is a city of contrasts: with new office blocks, slums and many strange and beautiful temples. It grew up on the River Menan and it used to have thousands of canals. Some people call it the Venice of the East.

Today, we plan on an even greater scale than Napoleon. Planners can design whole cities, not only their centres. And because they are so powerful, planners should think about the people who live in the places they have designed. What do *they* want?

Chandigarh in India was designed by a famous French architect, Le Corbusier. (See page 93). It is a beautiful city, and the Indians who live there are proud that it is so modern. But some of them feel sad about what they have lost. They miss the close-ness of an Indian street and often they alter the architect's design to fit in with their own way of life. Perhaps the best modern planning comes when the architect knows the people he is designing for and knows the way they want to live.

Bangkok is a different kind of city. It grew in the way it did because of where it is. Can you see how it follows the River Menan? There are many cities whose shape depends on the fact that they are on the coast, by a river or in a narrow gap in the hills.

4 The Place d'Etoile (Star Square) in Paris, now called the Place Charles de Gaulle. About 150 years ago, the tightly packed, medieval centre of the city was knocked down and architects began to rebuild it with long, wide streets and enormous squares.

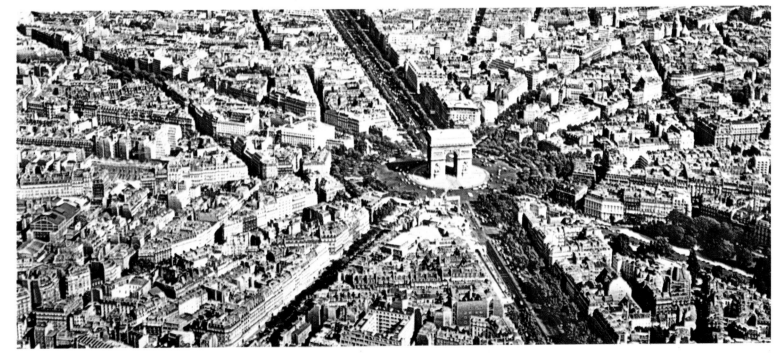

1 New York grew up during the Industrial Revolution. It is really five cities joined together, full of tall skyscrapers — a bit like a forest of cement.

Our biggest cities

Over a hundred years ago, man began seriously to make machines work for him. He began to build factories which produced much, much more than a simple workshop had ever been able to do. This was the start of what we call the Industrial Revolution. More and more people came from the countryside to work in the new industrial towns and there was little planning. Factories and houses grew up in

their thousands. Villages became towns and small towns grew into cities. And the cities themselves began swallowing up all the little towns and villages around them. This has happened, for example, in New York, Tokyo and London.

Today, we are trying to design our big cities much more carefully, with plenty of green park areas, so that they are better places to live in.

2 Tokyo, the capital of Japan, is the largest city in the world. It has no special plan and schools, flats and factories are all mixed up together.

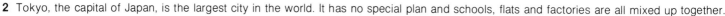

1 The People's House, in Brussels, built by the architect Victor Horta. It has an iron structure.

2 The Chandigarh Parliament Building in East Punjab, India, made from reinforced concrete, was designed by the famous French architect, Le Corbusier. Le Corbusier laid out the whole of the new city of Chandigarh.

The technical revolution

As towns grew bigger, men had to work out ways of making houses where all these extra people could live.

Obviously they needed to build bigger: but bricks alone were not strong enough for the tall buildings they had in mind. So they discovered how to use iron as a framework. But iron is brittle and heavy and it was not long before they discovered how to refine the iron to make steel which is many times stronger and lighter. Without steel, most of our highrise buildings would be impossible.

Many kinds of plastics were developed, with all their thousands of uses, reinforced concrete and glass, which had always been made in tiny sheets could now be made by the mile.

One invention which was especially important was the lift. This meant that for the first time man could build skyscrapers for everyone to use.

3 The Seagram Building in New York, designed by Mies van der Rohe. All the glass is tinted.

4 Habitat 1976 in Montreal, planned by Moshe Safdie, is made up of lots of prefabricated houses put on top of each other.

Houses where nobody lives

1 This is the Kailasa temple in Ellora, India. It is one of the most incredible technical achievements in the world because it was completely dug out of a mountain. Krishna II ordered it to be built, but even he was amazed when he saw it and, so the story goes, exclaimed, "This could only have been done by magic!"

2 Besides Kailasa, there are 33 caves in the mountains of Ellora, and each one is a temple.

Temples dug out of the rock

When we talk about houses, we mean all the buildings in a town or village. But many of these buildings are not homes, they are places for everyone; for example, churches, halls, schools and cinemas. This chapter is going to be about buildings like these, starting with the ancient temples.

People feel that their churches or temples are so important to them that they usually build them where they can be seen all over the town or village. Years ago, before radio and newspapers, people depended on church bells to warn them of danger and in many towns the square in front of the church is still used as a meeting place.

Some of the very old temples were marvellous buildings, at once magnificent and mysterious. It is often hard now for us to imagine how the workmen, artists and craftsmen could work so long and so hard to build them.

Perhaps among the most amazing are the temples at Ellora, in India. Temples like this which have been carved out of the rock can be found in China, Japan and Egypt.

3 One of the temples at Ellora with its finely decorated pillars.

4 Another temple with a beautifully carved statue of Buddha.

1 The Piazza dei Miracoli in Pisa, Italy. In this beautiful green square are the Baptistry, the Cathedral and the famous Leaning Tower.

2 The Temple of Concord at Agrigento in Sicily was built by the Greeks on a cliff.

3 Nôtre Dame in Paris was built on an island in the River Seine.

4 An Arab mosque in Nain, Iran. It is covered in brilliantly coloured ceramics.

Temples all over the world

All over the world, men and women believe in a religion, and they have done so as far back as anyone knows. Many, many hundreds of years ago most people believed that there were lots of gods and that they were like men, only much more powerful. Therefore, people had to make sure that the gods did not get angry and they gave them all kinds of presents and built great temples to please them. People believed in gods of lightning, rain, rivers, the sun, the moon and stars and many, many more.

If it seemed to people that their gods were not always as kind as they would like, at least these gods were normally their friends. On the other hand, people believed that there were also evil spirits, who

5 The Egyptians built huge temples like this one in Luxor. The two main statues are 16 m. high.

6 The Temple of the Sky in Peking, China. It has three beautiful domes in blue majolica, which is a kind of glazed pottery ware.

7 The Horyuji Temple in Nara, Japan, is perhaps one of the oldest wooden buildings in the world.

were not friendly at all. Look at the guardian in fig. 8. He is there to frighten away bad spirits.

Sometimes people told stories about their gods to explain things they did not understand about the world around them. For example, the Greeks thought that the sun was a marvellous chariot driven across the sky by a god every day. There are hundreds of strange and exciting stories like this, from every part of the world and we are still creating them. We call them *myths*.

Today, for most people there is only one God, although of course there are still many different beliefs and different religions.

8 This is a green demon, guarding one of the beautiful temples in Bangkok, Thailand.

9 This is a house of the *tiki*, the Polynesian gods. It has been built on the sea shore to be near to them.

10 This church in Antigua in Guatemala, is dedicated to Our Lady of Mercy. You can just see that it is on the edge of the city's main square.

1 Harrods is a big store in London. This picture was taken at Christmas time, so the store is covered with lights.

2 This is another big store, this time in Paris. It is called *Printemps*, which means "springtime". See the beautiful stairway, wide enough for lots of shoppers.

More buildings that aren't homes

Although everyone wants to have a home to live in, they also need places where they can go and meet other people. Churches and temples are important public buildings, but there are many others. Most of them have a special purpose — like a railway station — and they are used by so many people that they have a character all of their own which is not at all like a home.

Shops are planned for people in a special way. They are built to tempt people to come and buy. That is why they usually have big windows full of interesting and attractive things.

A town hall is where everything to do with life in the town is organized. People go there to sort out all kinds of day-to-day difficulties and sometimes even for public meetings and dances.

Government buildings are rather like important town halls. They deal with much more serious problems which are affecting the whole country.

All airports and stations have a place for people to wait. They usually have cafes too, to make the time pass more quickly for travellers and notice boards to let everyone know what is happening.

3 Behind these glass windows is the University Library at Cambridge in England.

4 This is the Town Hall of Hilversum in Holland, designed by Willem Dudock.

5 This strange and beautiful building is the Guggenheim Museum in New York, designed by the famous American architect Frank Lloyd Wright. Inside, it has a huge circular walkway which makes it look a bit like a sea-shell. It is full of modern paintings and sculptures.

6 Finland House in Helsinki, the capital of Finland, designed by Alvar Aalto.

7 The Mondadori printing works in Segrate, Italy.

8 The TWA terminal at the John F. Kennedy airport, New York, designed by the Finnish architect Eero Saarinen.

9 This is the Sports Arena in Rome, designed by the Italian architect, Pier Luigi Nervi. It has a dome of reinforced concrete, held up by huge concrete pillars.

10 The outside of the great Olympic swimming pool, built in Tokyo, and designed by the Japanese architect, Tange. ▷

Factories

People began to use machines in large numbers in the Industrial Revolution. But because the idea was new to them, they did not realize exactly what a machine age was going to mean. They were not ready for the way invention followed invention and one machine could make a thousand others. Sometimes it was hard to see if man was controlling machines or the other way about!

In the early days, people were excited by all the promises new machines held out to them. They could do things which for hundreds of years had seemed impossible. Films, radio, cars, X-rays, aeroplanes all looked a bit like magic. Machines would also do things *fast*; because iron and steel do not get tired in the same way that human beings do. Suddenly people saw that instead of a craftsman making a table in a month, a machine could do it in a day. A machine could also make things exactly the same, time after time. No longer was everything individually made, it could be built up of lots of little bits and each one could be replaced when it wore out. This meant that things could be cheaper. The idea of *mass production* had arrived. Try and think how life would be without machines. Think of all the things you take for granted which would not be there without them. Would you be sorry?

At that time, most people did not seem to see that machines make good servants but bad masters. They also did not realize that there was a price to pay for rushing ahead. They built factories full of machines without thinking about the men, women and children who were going to have to operate them. These people had a very miserable time. They worked long hours in cramped, horrible places and many became tired and ill. Worse still, more and more people crowded into the cities and no one planned how they were going to live. Today we have to pay for this, because many of our industrial towns were planned for factories and not for people. People are trying out all kinds of plans now, but it is difficult to grow grass once you have sown concrete and even more difficult to remake a city when the people are already there.

But not all factories are bad places by any means. Today, some are very clean, pleasant places to work. Can you think of any ways they could be made even better? A lot of people are bored in a factory because they have to do the same thing over and over again. How could their work be made more interesting?

1 This looks a bit like a camping site but it is a school in Cergy-Pontoise in France. Here children are both playing and working.

2 An open-air school in China.

School

What is school? You try and answer. People say it is a place where children go to find out, not only facts like "what is the capital of Italy?" (Rome, in case you are wondering) but all sorts of things like what they want to be when they grow up. Maybe it should also be a place where people want to be and where, on the whole, they are happy. But ideas are one thing and what really happens is another.

Perhaps you have been bored in school. Everyone has — unless they aren't being quite truthful. Sometimes it is because you aren't interested in the lesson; but sometimes it isn't your fault and it isn't the fault of the teacher. It is to do with the way your school is organized. Some schools have far too many children in each class. Some schools have tiny, noisy classrooms, with hardly any space to play. Some schools are so spread out that the children spend a long time walking between classrooms and it is hard for them all to know each other. Can you think of any ways your school could be improved? Of course, no one can help a lot of the things that are wrong, but it is good to imagine sometimes how we would like things to be. On these pages are some children who are lucky enough to go to schools which they like very much indeed. Look at the school at Charenton (figs. 5,6 and 7) where there are lots of things, from the fountains to the classrooms which are unusual and fun.

3 This school in Bergamo, Italy, is very unusual. See how it has been painted blue, green and white. It looks very cool.

4 Another open-air school, this time in Africa.

5, 6 & 7 These are three photos of Nôtre-Dame des Missions in Charenton, France. This was a convent, before it was converted into a school by Claude Franck. The doors and stairways are all sorts of unusual shapes and you can see from one classroom into another. There are mirrors, too, and fountains to play in.

In some countries, not everyone gets the chance to go to school, and those who do feel lucky! Often, girls especially are expected to stay at home instead. In fig. 4, these children may well have come a long way to this class.

In fig. 8, there is a plan of a school designed by two architects with the help of ten children. Would you like a school like this? Or do you like your own better?

8 This is a plan of a school seen from above, worked out by two architects, Eduardo Alamaro and Anna Liguori, with the help of ten children from Naples, in Italy.

1 Mick and his friends drew a school in a park. Would you like an open-air school?

Why not invent your own school?

Here are some schools designed by children, 7 to 10 years old. Why don't you try? Of course, you can't really build a school yet, but you go to one and you must have ideas about what you like and what you don't like. Maybe, when you stop going to school, you will forget your ideas if you don't put them down.

One of the planners' biggest difficulties is getting everyone to agree. Try out your ideas on your

2 Philip wanted a school with walls you can see through.

3 Lisa and her friends want a school with a zoo. Can you see the giraffe?

4 Jenny and her friends want a school in an enormous circus tent. She also wants a fountain like an elephant.

5 Jim's ideal school is inside a mountain.

friends and see if they like them too. Do you want lots of equipment — books, paper, filmshows and toys; or would you prefer somewhere to swim, or even a small farm with ponies, cats and dogs for you to look after? Most of these children planned to have trees, flowers or animals. But perhaps you would rather go to a space-age school inside a huge glass bubble.

6 Mark would like a school laid out like a merry-go-round in the middle of a wood.

7 Jack likes this garden school, where the children can paint out-of-doors.

8 Polly and her friends want a school near a lake with lots of animals.

9 Max and his friends want a school in a garden with a pool full of coloured fish.

10 Anna designed her school like this because she likes basketball.

Play space

The white cat

1 Once upon a time there was a white cat, who lived in a pretty, pink house in the middle of quiet hills and valleys. The only noise came from the railway, but it was an old line and no one used it much.

2 Then, one spring, someone decided to build a station in the village. Other houses grew up too, because it was a nice village and now that they could reach it easily, more people wanted to live there.

3 Spring turned to summer and even more people visited the village. "Very suitable," said a smart man in a dark suit. But for what, no one knew. Life went on as usual and the white cat sunned herself peacefully in the ripening corn.

4 Autumn came and it was time to dig the parsnips and potatoes. No one paid much attention to the trucks in the field and the men, cutting down the trees. They had begun to get used to the sound of engines and machinery. You can't see the cat because it's too misty.

5 With winter, came a sudden and amazing change. The trains now brought long, long strings of goods wagons; and there were two huge black things squatting in the field. "Storage tanks," said someone who knew more than the rest. "It's for the oil refinery they're building. Now we'll see all sorts of new things in the village!"

6 Then it was time to plough the fields again. The white cat sniffed the fresh earth. But with the spring came a lot of strange new buildings, all smooth shapes, concrete and glass. At first, people were interested in them, and children liked to watch the bulldozers and new, fast cars. But somehow, there wasn't as much room as before. "All these new people," said one old man, sadly, "and I don't know any of them."

7 Summer came, and still more cranes and trucks. Fences went up and concrete spread and spread. The white cat sat miserably on the trunk of her favourite tree. It would never grow again. Her house was being pulled down and the green fields outside her home had almost disappeared.

8 It must be Autumn in the new town. It's hard to tell. Harder still to see where the old village is, and the fields are now a four-lane motorway. There is no lake for the children to play in, only a small, cement park; and the white cat has disappeared for ever.

Where can you play?

There is something very exciting about a building site, and most people have at some time or another watched new houses, new flats or factories being built. There is always something happening. Perhaps it is the trucks arriving with cement, or huge iron girders being lifted into place. But it is depressing to think that all over the world, green grass and fields are being eaten up by cement.

Of course not all cities are bad places and in fact, many of us choose to live there. Usually there are many, many kinds of people in them, all with different ways and customs. It is exciting to see them and good to find out about other ways of living as well as our own. But sadly, the planners don't always think of ways to make life better in a city. Often, they don't have to live in the flats they design, or near the factories and motorways they have planned, and some plans which sound good in theory are a disaster, if everybody's special needs are not worked out. Sometimes this means that many people are dissatisfied. Often it means that play space disappears. As you can see from pages 106-7, there were plenty of places to play near the village at first. You could climb the trees, run races in the grass and skate on the pond in winter. But where could you play in fig 8?

These Hindu children have got space where they can play. They are having a great time in the surf.

Can you play in the street?

Cities are full of men, women and children. But are these cities made for them? Sometimes the tall skyscrapers put the pavements in shadow all through the day and there are so many people that they keep bumping into one another.

This is partly because cities grew so fast that no one thought enough about how all these people were going to live together. Planners thought about complex tower blocks and factories, but they didn't always think about simple things like how to make it pleasant to walk in the street.

The traffic, too, grew thicker, as more people came to the cities and this made matters worse. Too many cars and trucks can strangle a city, choking it with metal and exhaust fumes. Today, we are trying to block off some streets to cars to make them quieter, nicer places to be. Many cities now have fast, main roads for cars and pleasant shopping streets for people, where they can stand and talk and meet their friends.

1 This is an old photograph of a street in New York. Where could children play here?

2 This is a street in Tokyo, where the traffic has been blocked off. There are even places for people to sit.

3 This is a square in the old city of Venice. Two girls are skipping right in the middle. This is because there are no cars, trucks or motor bikes in Venice. Everyone travels on foot or by boat and there is plenty of space for children to play.

1 "Watch me!" This boy is showing how far he can jump in a play park in Los Angeles.

2 Flying must be rather like swinging — or is it the other way about? That's what these Hungarian children from Budapest think, anyway.

Play parks and adventure playgrounds

It doesn't take that much space to make a really good playground. But in most cities, how many places like this are there? And how often do you have to cross busy roads to reach them? Maybe you live in the country but even so, would you like to be able to go to some of the play parks and adventure playgrounds in these pictures whenever you wanted? What kind of play parks would you like best?

3 This marvellous whale was built for children on the beach in Israel.

4 This is a play park in Tokyo, Japan.

5 A camel and a little hut in an adventure playground in Hamburg, Germany.

How should our cities look?

Cities are made up of lots of different areas. In most cases, the areas have a distinct character, so that even if you don't know the city well, you can tell that you have moved from one part to another just by looking. There is the shopping area, with lots of big shops, the business area full of banks and office blocks, perhaps a special area around the docks, if the city is on a river or the sea-coast and maybe an area of theatres and concert halls. There are areas too, where there are a lot of people of one race or nationality — Chinese, Spanish, German or Italian, for example. This is because people naturally tend to stick together in a foreign country, perhaps because they are home-sick, or perhaps because it is nice to hear their own language spoken around them. These different areas bring a lot of colour and life into a city.

There is also another kind of area, and this is often a little more difficult to spot. It is generally a little way out from the centre of the city and it is usually a little like a village; with its own shops, schools and post office. This is probably because it *was* once a village, before the city grew and swallowed it up. Of course the village changed as it became part of the city and the people took different jobs as their land turned into streets and buildings. But mostly, they still lived near each other and knew one another.

Things rarely stay the same for ever and often these little houses are knocked down to make way for huge skyscrapers. When this happens, these small villages-in-cities disappear. You can see this happening in the picture below. The little houses have a few gardens. The people living there can see

1 This is the old Italian quarter of Buenos Aires, capital of Argentina. Can you see how the skyscrapers are towering above it? They look as if they are about to take it over.

112

one another from their houses. But if they lived at the top of a skyscraper, it would be a very different matter.

This is one of the big problems of cities; too many skyscrapers can completely rub out an area. The character dies. Sometimes it's because the tall blocks are offices and people are only there during the day and at night they leave the streets empty. Even if the skyscrapers are flats, the people have probably come from many different places and they do not know one another. Worse still, they will certainly work all over the city, sometimes miles away and there is not much chance for them to meet. The feeling of a village has been lost and people don't have the same sense of belonging.

Even for children it is not always easy to play amongst multi-storey buildings. A lot of children think they make their city boring. Do you think so?

But not all big blocks of flats are ugly. There are many which are very pleasant places to live. Planners have tried to work out ways to use space to its best advantage, because that is one of the difficulties of living in a city — there is not much room for everyone. In some places they have built gardens on the roof tops, in others they have made beds and chairs that fold away, or whole kitchens in cupboards. Can you think of any other ways in which you could make more space to live in?

Below you can see very clearly what these three children think is wrong with their city. They live in Genoa in Italy, in an area of traffic and highrise flats and they have drawn first how they live, and second how they would like to live. Have you ever seen anywhere you would really not like to live?

2, 3 & 4 In these three drawings, three children from Genoa show first how they live, and then how they would like to live.

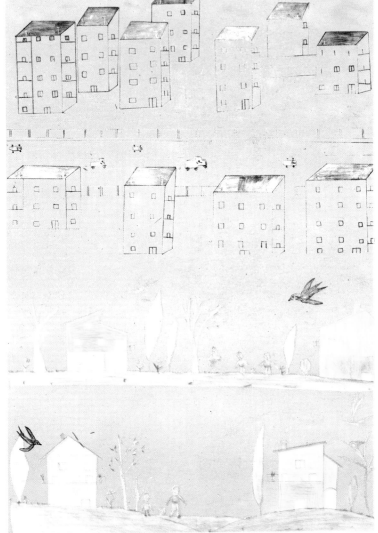

Cities of the future

The population of the world is growing at an amazing rate. This is a crowd at a festival in India and it gives you some idea of what it would be like if our numbers keep on increasing in the way they are now. It may seem strange, but the population grows fastest where there is least food and money, like India. What can we do to help everyone have enough to live on?

1 A garden city Fifty years ago, when the famous American architect, Frank Lloyd Wright, planned this city called Broadacre, nobody worried about overpopulation. Wright believed that industrial cities were not the best way for people to live and so he put his ideal city in the middle of green fields. Space was unlimited and each family had its own house and — of course — its own car. Do you think it would be possible to build a city like this today?

Architects' cities of the future

There are so many people in the world that we simply can't picture them all. There are four thousand million of us.

Are you surprised? Maybe not, because it is hard even to imagine a number that big. This number is getting larger every day and in India alone, over twelve million babies are born every year. Try to imagine twelve million dinners — and they are needed *every day*. Then you begin to see the size of the problem. In fact, some experts are worried that in two hundred years time there will not be enough for everyone to eat, there will be few raw materials, like copper and iron, and we shall all be living in an enormous suburb of some world city. It is a very frightening thought.

But not everyone believes this. For one thing, it is hard to work out exactly how fast our population is growing because it is not growing everywhere at the same rate. Oddly enough, poor countries like Asia and South America are growing much more quickly than rich ones. Perhaps this is because these people

have to put all their faith in their children and the future, because their present life is so unpleasant. Certainly, in America where there is ten times the amount of food that there is in India, the population is hardly growing at all. It is also true, that people are continually thinking up new materials and new ways of using old ones and that should help us to feed some of the new people coming into the world.

But one thing is certain. We cannot go on thinking that the earth has an endless supply of the things we need. Once upon a time if we wanted something new, we just threw the old one away. Now we are beginning to see that we must be more careful. Trees, animals and plants all need time to grow.

Look at the plans on the next two pages. These are all ways people have invented to live in our modern world. Would you like to live in any of these cities? Some of the ideas are actually being used today, although perhaps not in the way that the architects expected.

2   A city in the desert The Italian architect Paolo Soleri thought that a good place for a city would be where very few people are living at present. He chose the desert. This isn't such an odd choice as it looks, because we believe that many years ago a lot of our deserts were green and fertile. It is only because the climate became hotter and drier that few things now grow there. Soleri decided that a system of dams and canals could soon change all that. Mesa City is made up of thirty-four villages, all connected to each other.

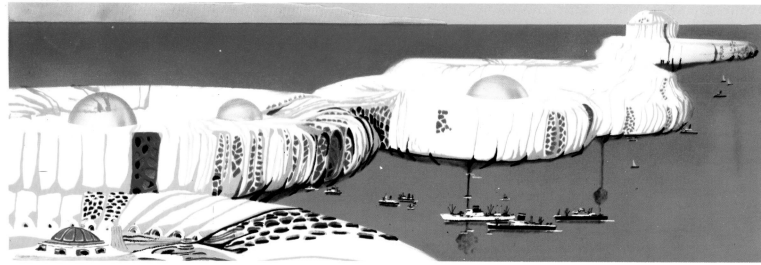

3   A floating city The American architect, William Katavolos, thought along the same lines. "If the world is becoming overpopulated," he said, "we must go on the sea where there is plenty of space." His floating city is made out of a new kind of plastic which goes hard when it touches water. The artificial islands which make up the city are all connected with each other.

4   An underground city The French architect, Edouard Utudjian, decided that in his city, all the factories, cars and railways should go underground, leaving the people to live on the surface. Here there would be no roads, only woods and fields. Although we do not go this far yet, there are lots of cities today with railways and even roads underground.

5 Funnel city This idea was thought up by the Swiss architect, Walter Jonas. He thought that in order to leave as much room as possible on the ground for trees and fields, cities should be narrow at the bottom and wide at the top. These strange funnels would be about 300 ft. high. Maybe it would feel rather odd, living with all those people and cars on top of you!

6 A hanging city The French architect, Paul Maymont, was more worried about ruining the old cities than finding new places to live. Instead of building skyscrapers, he planned huge suspended platforms. These would look rather like huge fir trees, loaded with thousands of people, shops, flats and offices. Each platform would be connected to the next and to the old city with a bridge.

7 A walking city This is perhaps one of the strangest ideas and it was invented by the English architect, Ron Herron. There would be one capital of the world, which he planned as a huge engine. The other cities would look like large machines on gigantic mechanical legs, which would take them wherever they were needed.

1 Termites, rather like ants, live in large nests made of earth. Each nest is nearly 4 m. high, and contains many thousands of termites.

2 In a crack in the middle of this underwater rock, you can just see the eye of an octopus in his hole.

3 Weaving sparrows actually weave their nests out of grass. These nests are beautifully made with a little opening in the side where the birds can come in and out. They are in the shape of a ball and are carefully lined inside.

Animals need homes

Most animals need homes just as humans do and although they are of course very different to ours, they are often extraordinary pieces of engineering. Just like man, animals need somewhere they can be safe, both from the weather and from their enemies. They especially need somewhere to protect their children. There are two main ways they can do this: they can camouflage their homes, in other words make them blend in with the background; or they can build them in places where other animals either can't or don't want to reach them.

4 Blackbirds make nests like little bowls. They glue the mud, twigs and earth together with spit and these nests are so firm and strong that they could be used for several years running.

5 Dormice live in little nests where they keep warm through the winter. This is when they *hibernate*. During the summer, when there is plenty of food, they eat as much as they can. Then, when the frosts arrive, they curl up and sleep until spring, warm and safe with their protective layer of fat.

6 Foxes dig holes, where they and their cubs keep safe. They hunt at night for rabbits, mice, small birds and animals. If they can get in, they will raid the farmer's hen coop and perhaps their worst enemy is man.

Skylarks hardly build a nest at all; it is often just a collection of twigs and grass on the ground; but it fits in perfectly with the grassland where they like to live. Badgers however, have a very permanent home. They live in a sett, which is like a huge, beautifully made burrow and sometimes the same sett is used for many, many generations. Badgers are peaceful creatures and sometimes they have 'lodgers' — a fox or even a family of rabbits will often share their large home.

Badgers usually find their homes ready-made.

But beavers actually build their own dams. These tangled masses of branches and twigs are very skilfully constructed and often block the river so well that it floods. Their homes are called *lodges* and are built to keep the young beavers safe.

Perhaps one of the oddest homes belongs to a fish, The mother fish keeps her babies (called *fry*) in her mouth whenever danger threatens, until they are big enough to manage for themselves.

These are only a few of the ways animals live. Look around you and you will see many more.

7 These jackal cubs are waiting for their mother to bring them something to eat. They look rather like wolf cubs, and like wolves, they can occasionally be tamed. Jackals live alone or in couples and they do not dig a permanent home of their own. They live in holes they find in the ground or in the rocks.

Cities in outer space

So far, we have only been talking about this earth. But who knows; if there are people on other worlds, how do they live? Do they have fantastic houses and beautiful gardens? Do they have the same problems as we have, or perhaps do they have difficulties of their own which are just as bad if not worse? Perhaps one day we will be able to travel to worlds far outside our own and discover whether some of the amazing facts that scientists and astronomers tell us are true. But distances in space are so enormous it is hard even to think of how we will do it. Do you know, if you don't count the sun (which is, of course, a star), the nearest star is two light years away? That means its light takes two years to reach us. And light travels at 186,000 miles per second.

In the picture below, you can see an imaginary city from another world. Why not try and make your own?

You can make this space city out of anything you have at hand — jam jars, candles, straws, egg boxes and toothpicks, cardboard, polystyrene, or any sort of packing material. In this city, the spacemen and monsters are models.

Looking inside a house

1 The woman you can see fetching water from this beautifully painted well is called Stefania Voncigniska. She lives in Zalipia, a village in Poland. Stefania lives alone, but her son lives in a nearby village and he comes to see her every Saturday. The village people in this part of Poland nearly always paint lovely patterns both inside and outside their houses.

2 Stefania has painted a sort of patterned sunflower outside her house.

A painted house

It is rather like exploring to go into a house for the first time, especially if you have never met the person who lives there. You don't know quite what you will find except that everything will tell you a little about that person. Inside their houses people keep things they like and things that mean a lot to them.

Up until now you have looked at the outsides of houses, and the way people live in them; but you haven't really seen inside a house. After all, the outsides of houses are mostly for looking at — people actually live inside them. Maybe houses are a bit like faces — you need a door to go in them and windows to give you light, just as a face has eyes and a mouth. In fact, most houses do have an expression if you look at them.

But of course it is inside a house that people eat, sleep and have their own things. This chapter shows what the insides of lots of houses look like, beginning with a beautifully painted cottage in Poland.

3 This is Stefania's cellar, where she keeps her wine. She has painted bunches of grapes on the door as well as carrots, onions and cherries.

4 Stefania is looking after her animals. She has painted all kinds of peacocks, chickens and little birds on the outside of the stable.

5 Stefania has put the animals in the stable. Can you see the corn dolly hanging on the fence too? "Why don't you come into the house?" she asks.

6 As she goes into the house she says, "Let's go into the kitchen. It's cooler in there and I can make us something to eat."

7 Stefania is making soup and it soon smells delicious. "I am on my own a lot," she tells us, "and so I have plenty of time to paint — when I am not working on the farm, that is." The kitchen is her bedroom too.

8 Stefania goes out of the room. Can you see the painted ceiling and the pretty bunches of dried flowers?

9 "Come and see how I make the paints," she says.

10 Stefania begins making the paints. "First of all," she explains, "I take some coloured earth and then I mix it into a paste with milk, soapy water and the yolk of an egg."

Now you have seen all round Stefania's cottage. There are two bedrooms, one of which is also the kitchen and they are divided by a passage way. You can also see her big stove, which heats the cottage in the winter.

1 Here you can see inside a *dacha*, or cottage in a village near Moscow, the capital of the Soviet Union. On the right is a beautiful wooden door, and in the room behind, there is a bed with piles of cushions on it. To the left, you can just see the stove which is long and low. The villagers sleep by their stoves in winter, when it is very cold indeed.

2 This bedroom belongs to an artist who lives in New York. He made all the furniture himself. He has hung the bed from the ceiling so that it is like a huge swing.

3 This straw hut belongs to a family of the Wakamba tribe, who live in the forests of Kenya, in Africa. There are no beds, table or any other furniture and the floor is covered with soft leaves.

Inside houses all over the world

These houses are from different parts of the world, but they all have one thing in common. They have all been decorated by the people who live in them. The reason for this is that it tells you a great deal more about someone if you see what he or she has chosen to have in their house.

Too many buildings are anonymous. They have no special character because no one in particular cares for them. Of course, houses in any place vary as much as the people who live in them and these here are only a few examples. You have to remember too, that not everyone in Africa or Asia lives in the same sort of way. There are also people living in these places in houses not so very different from those in Europe or America. But these ones here do give you some idea of the great variety there is in ways of living and they are also interesting and pretty to look at.

4 This is a house in the village of Cobombo, in Nubia, near the River Nile. You are looking at the sitting room which has been painted with vases of flowers. This is where the people who live here entertain their visitors.

5 This is a mud house in Rajasthan, which is a state in India. The roof is made of bales of straw. The people who live in this part of the world are often so poor that they don't have enough to eat; but this family doesn't look at all sad.

6 This Chinese house belongs to a family from the country around Hangchow. In the middle of the room, there is a very strange bed. It is made up of cupboards and drawers, each one painted and lacquered with scenes of people, boats and houses. The people who live here have spent many years building their house and they are very proud of it.

7 This is a house in Puglia, in the south of Italy. The whitewashed stone walls are re-painted every time they get a little dingy and they look beautifully clean and cool even in the middle of summer, when it is very hot. This house has only one room, where the people who live here entertain their visitors, cook, eat and sleep. At night, they draw a pretty coloured curtain to make part of the room into a bedroom.

8 This house belongs to an artist in Bosna, which is a village in Nepal in Asia. The men who are busy painting are sitting cross-legged on divans. Above them, you can just see eight pictures by the artist. They are so full of people and scenes that they look like complicated patterns. Below, there is an altar dedicated to Buddha, and on it there are lots of little statues. These have a special meaning; they mean that in this house, the people are trying to reach perfection through their painting.

9 Now we are near Venezuela and Brazil, in a country called Guyana. It is hard to believe but you are looking at the inside of a house. These hammocks belong to the Avayanasa Indians and they sling them under shelters. This is where they sleep at night and they rest here too, during the day if it gets too hot.

10 This is a house in Sanaa, the capital of the Yemen and a rich sheikh lives here with his son. A sheikh is an important Arabian ruler. The son is smoking a narghile, which is a sort of water pipe. Tobacco smoke passes first through scented water, which makes it deliciously cool and sweet-smelling, and then it is sucked out through a long pipe. Can you see how richly the cushions are embroidered and the narghiles are beautifully decorated as well. Notice the guns, too. But they are not for decoration!

11 Isn't this girl beautiful? She lives in an Indian village in the forests of the Amazon, in South America. Her family are hunters. The village is inside a huge, round, fenced-in space where all the families live together.

1 A poet's attic-room, painted by Hogarth.

2 Country children in a cottage, by the French painter, Fragonard.

3 This painting of a scholar by Rembrandt shows the inside of a Dutch house over three hundred years ago.

4 Here you can see a girl serving *polenta* (a sort of Italian porridge), painted by the Italian, Pietro Longhi.

5 In this Chinese print you can see a boy and girl talking in a brightly-coloured Chinese house. Notice how tiny the girl's feet are. This was thought to be a sign of beauty and Chinese girls would bind their feet tightly to stop them growing.

How we used to live: inside a house from long ago

Do you ever wonder what it must have been like to live a long time ago? It would be really interesting to know what people thought about their homes. It would be even more exciting to be able to see them, exactly as they were — but of course as they didn't have cameras, we can't do that.

What we can do is look at their paintings. In some ways that is even better, because an artist shows how he feels about what he is painting. A camera can only show what is in front of the lens.

Some things are perhaps hard to imagine; for example, what it would be like to live without electricity or running water; but many more things we can recognize very easily. Can you see the dogs and cats? The cat in fig 1 has found herself a comfortable spot, just as she would today.

6 This man sitting outside a little tent and writing, is called Balwant Singh. Long ago he was an Indian prince, but instead of fighting and feasting all the time as many of his friends did he was much happier listening to music, reading books and looking at all kinds of beautiful works of art. You can see the brushes he is using to write with, and his narghile. In the background a servant is waiting to cool him with a fan.

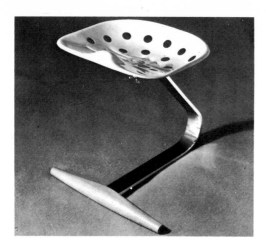

1 This stool designed by Castiglioni looks rather like a tractor seat.

2 An armchair like a giraffe, made by Albert Gebhard.

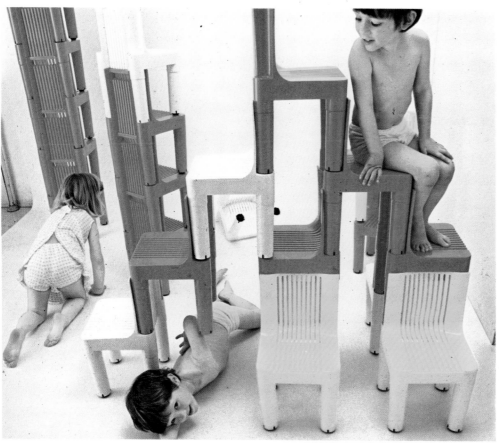

3 You can build a castle with these chairs designed by Marco Zanuso.

4 Stacy Dukes designed these little seats, called *Efebino*.

5 This armchair is really just a stuffed sack. It was designed by three Italian architects.

Furniture for everyone

Many years ago, people everywhere had to make their own furniture. In some parts of the world they still do. While this happens it means that every table, every bed is a bit different.

In many countries, people who were much cleverer with their fingers than the rest began making furniture for others. They were the craftsmen and once, every village used to have its carpenter and its stonemason, its potter or metal worker. This worked very well because these craftsmen made furniture which suited the customs and tastes of the people who used it.

The only difficulty was that it was slow; and of course only the rich could have much choice in what they wanted — indeed, have very much furniture at all.

Then came the machine age; and suddenly, everyone could have mass-produced things, knives, forks, plates and carpets; they all came out exactly the same. On the whole this was good, because things did not cost so much and many more people could have what had once only been for a very few. But it also meant that a small number of people decided what everyone was going to use. Mass production only works if everyone *does* use the same things and if you want something only slightly different from everyone else, you are likely to be disappointed.

Today, designers are making furniture especially for children; but not as yet in large numbers. Maybe one day it will be mass produced and you will be able to buy it anywhere.

1 Here are the forty pieces of M-game laid out on the ground. You can build masses of different things with them.

2 This could be a stage — or a slide. Or even a table.

Furniture you can play with

You might think that a chair is something just to sit on and a table is, well, a table. But new designers have been making furniture into a game that anyone can play and where you make up the rules as you go along. The furniture in the picture (which looks more like a big building set) is called M-game and was designed by Raffaella Vallecchi and Daryouch Hadijan. Each one of the forty pieces of wood is different and you can make forts and palaces, a stage or a shop. It just depends what you want.

3 The pieces of wood are easy to fix together. They slot into one another as you can see.

4 You can play all sorts of other games (like hide-and-seek) while you are building.

5 These children have made a very fine house. There is somewhere to eat, somewhere to sleep and somewhere just to sit.

1 Here is a cat fast asleep on a sofa in the sun. On top of the cat is a kitten. Cats like sleeping, especially when it's warm.

2 Look. The kitten isn't really asleep. A fly buzzes in to the room. He opens one eye and then the other and he blinks. "What's that?"

The kitten who walked by himself

Perhaps you've got a kitten, so you know they are always getting into trouble. Maybe it's because they just want to find out about everything.

3 He climbs onto the table. "I wonder what *this* is?" he thinks as he pats a grape.

4 "Is it good to eat?" And he bites it just a little, to taste. "Ugh! Not ripe yet!"

5 "Maybe there's something more interesting here." He sniffs a pot of glue. "Hmm. I don't think I'll try *that*."

6 "But what are they?" He pokes a jar of paint brushes. "What are they for?"

7 Crash! The paint brush falls on the table. "I was only looking, honestly! In fact, I wasn't there at all! I don't even like paint brushes!"

8 Silence. No one comes. "It's safe to go on exploring. Maybe I'll have a look at that shelf."

9 "All these vases and things. A bit boring, really. I'll just have a scratch."

10 "Help! What's that? A small man with a stick!" His tail twitches and his fur stands up on end. "I'll be brave. He's not very big."

11 He jumps closer. "Whew! It's only one of those plaster things." He sticks his tongue out. "Afraid of me, probably."

12 "Let's move on. Leaves? Yes, and growing too. Not much good, really. Don't know why they bother with them."

13 "There must be *something* up here. After all, they always try to stop me climbing up these shelves. Come to think of it, it's quite difficult."

14 "How do I get down?" He puts out one paw. "Shall I wake her up and ask her?"

15 "Whoops!" Thump. "That's one way of doing it. Is she going to be mad at me?"

16 "No, thank goodness. Too hot, probably. Maybe I'll just cat nap for a bit. It *is* rather warm." And they both go to sleep.

Dolls houses

This isn't exactly a doll's house, but you can look inside and see everything the family is doing. Is it anything like your house? It belongs to Mr Kit E. Katte and his wife Clara.

smoke

chimney

weathercock

roof

television aerial

attic

large boxes

suitcase

gutter

chest of drawers

trunk

rocking horse

eaves

drawings

curtain

toy box

bathroom cupboard

mirror

table

bath

pillow

Leo

towels

window

eiderdown

bed

basin

bedside table

Liza

train

stool

grandfather clock

television

clothes hooks

standard lamp

vase

hood

piano

sink

umbrellas

Mrs Katte

armchair

Miss Paws

stove

table cloth

front door

carpet

axe

tiles

logs

barrow

hat

steering wheel

Mr Kit E. Katte

headlight

flowers

car door

rake

wheel

radiator

spade

inner tube

screwdriver

jack

pump

tortoise

1 This is a little dolls' house made in France when your grandparents were children.

Dolls' houses from long ago

You have now seen all kinds of houses that people are living in or have lived in. On the next few pages you can see some houses which were never intended for people at all, although they have everything in them that people might want. They are dolls' houses — but they are not only for dolls. Toy soldiers could live there, little animals, anyone, as long as they were small enough. Most of them were made a very long time ago and you can see, just as you did in the paintings, the sort of things that the people who made them had in their houses. In the living room and the bedroom on page 138, there is a little grandfather clock and all the furniture is made of wood. In one of the shops, you can see the beautiful jars where people used to keep goods.

Do you like houses like this? Adults certainly do. Look how much trouble they took to make them not only for children, but for themselves as well.

2 You can open it. See how pretty it is inside, with its sofa, chairs and the little white stove. There are even some bowls on the table.

1 This story is about a little girl called Jade, who had a room all to herself in this house. When it was hot, she would sit on the stairs outside the house and watch everyone going past in the street.

Jade looks for her mother

This story about a little doll has been made up by collecting together dolls' houses from Italy, France, Germany, Vietnam and Peru, because people make dolls' houses all over the world — and not only houses. There are castles, circuses, shops, stations and even garages. Of course, if you wanted, you could make up all kinds of stories about just one of these houses.

2 At school, her teacher said: "For homework, I want everyone to ask their mother to help them with something they like doing. Tell me about it tomorrow morning."

3 On the way home, Jade thought about her homework. "I know," she said. "I'll ask for a box of chocolates, and we can eat them together."

4 She ran into the kitchen. But her mother wasn't there. And she wasn't in the living room either.

5 She went into the bedroom. No one there. Jade felt a bit cross. She really did want to get started on her homework.

6 "She's gone shopping," decided Jade, and she ran out into the street. She looked in the shop where her mother bought tea. But she wasn't there.

7 Then she looked in the sweet shop. Perhaps her mother was already buying chocolates? But she wasn't there either.

8 Then she came to a very strange house at the end of the street. Jade was a bit scared, because she knew it was a magic house, but she went in.

9 Inside there were two strange, fat men. "Take a chance, have a dance," they said. "I think you're silly," said Jade. But she waited until she was near the door before she said it.

10 She went down the street, until she came to the house where her mother's best friend lived. The door was open, so she slipped in.

11 Her mother's friend was sitting in the living room, singing a lullabye to her baby. But she hadn't seen Jade's mother.

12 "Is that you, Jade?" called Maria. "Come upstairs!" Maria was Jade's friend, so she ran into the bedroom to see her.

13 They played on the see-saw. Then Jade said, "I'm looking for Mummy." "She was in the hat shop," said Maria.

14 The lady in the hat shop told her, "Your mother has gone to the dance. You must go too!" And she gave Jade a beautiful hat to wear.

15 Jade's mother was very pleased to see her. "Have a chocolate," she said. "I think I like dancing even better than chocolates," said Jade. "I'll have to tell them all about it tomorrow, at school."

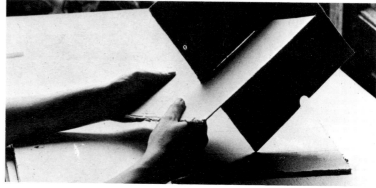

A dolls' house made out of three pieces of cardboard **1** Cut three squares of cardboard, 30 cm. wide. In the middle of two of them, make a cut, half way up.

2 Take the two pieces with slits in them and slip one into the other crossways. Now stand them in the middle of the third piece. Glue them or fix them in place with sticky tape. Your house now has four rooms. See page 143 for how to make the furniture.

How to make a dolls' house

It is not as difficult as you might think to decorate a dolls' house. You can use all kinds of bits and pieces. It only needs little thought and imagination to transform a scrap of wrapping paper into wallpaper, or an acorn cup into a little bowl.

It is a good idea to keep a box for collecting things which might come in useful — broken toys, a pretty stamp, tin foil or bits of twig or plastic, for example.

The actual house is more complicated. If you are not lucky enough to find someone to help you make it out of wood, you can make all kinds of interesting houses yourself out of cardboard boxes, fruit boxes or old packing cases.

3 Here is a bathroom where a mother is giving her baby a bath. There are two bathroom cupboards as well, and she keeps the baby's bottle in one of them. There is also a little toilet.

4 This is a bedroom. This little girl is in bed but she isn't asleep yet. There is a pretty flowery wallpaper made from wrapping paper and she has a stamp stuck on the wall for a picture. Can you see her wardrobe, too?

5 There is another bedroom. The little girl's elder sister, called Vanessa, is looking for her cat in the wardrobe. "Where *is* he?" she's saying. "He's always on my bed!"

6 This is the kitchen. Vanessa isn't cooking, she's sharpening her pencils so she can draw a picture. She is very good at drawing.

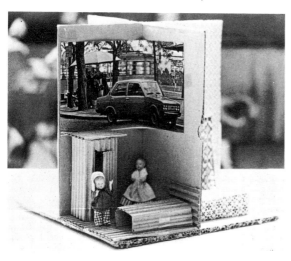

A dolls' house made out of a long box **1** If you can find a long box (a shoe box is good for this), you can make a house with all the rooms in a row. First of all, take off the lid. Then cut the edge off the lid, so you are left with a flat piece of cardboard. Now cut it into three or four pieces. These are going to be your walls.

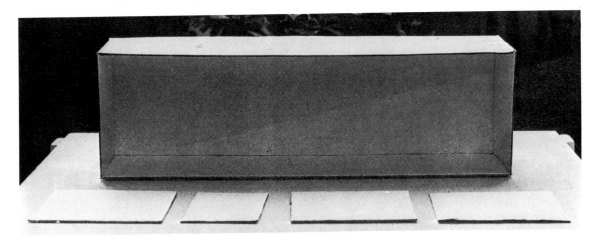

2 Next, slip the pieces of cardboard into the box as you see here, fixing them firmly with sticky tape if necessary. Now you have made your rooms all in a row. If you want them to connect with one another cut a little door in each piece of cardboard before you slot it into the box. The furniture for this little house is made out of cut corks. (See page 143)

Another dolls' house from a box **1** Perhaps you can find a box already divided into compartments. (Some fruit boxes are like this.) This means that the rooms are already made for you. In fact you may have to take some of the divisions out, otherwise you will have too many rooms. Stand the box on end and make it firm so it won't fall over. Now wallpaper the rooms with wrapping paper or whatever you have at hand. The mirror is made from a button covered with silver paper. (See page 142 for the furniture.)

2 On the right, you can see the front of the house. This is made out of the lid of the box. If the box doesn't have a lid, cut out a piece of cardboard the same size as the box. Make two little holes with a pin one third and two thirds up on the left hand side about 10mm from the edge. Make two holes in the box exactly the same height on the left hand side and also about 10mm from the edge. Then pass a piece of string through the holes in the box and the holes in the cardboard and tie them together. Do the same on the other side. Now you can open and close your house by tying and untying the string. I don't quite know how the kitten got in here, but he seems to like it.

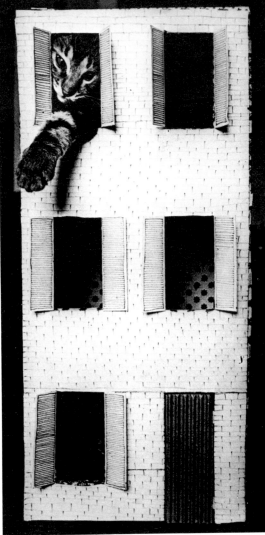

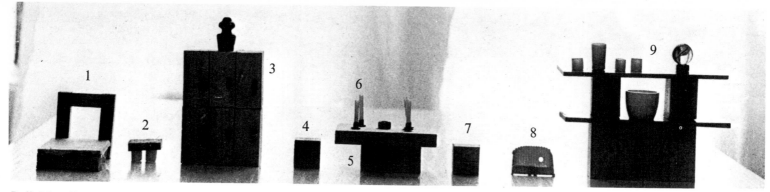

Dolls' furniture 1 Here you can see some of the furniture from the house where the kitten was playing. This is how it was made. (1) the bed is a small block of wood with another thinner bit of wood at the end. (2) the stool is made from a strip of cork stuck on two little bits of plasticine. (3) the cupboard is a block of wood with doors drawn in with a felt-tip pen. You can stick on little bits of plasticine for door handles. (4, 7) the two little stools are cubes of wood painted different colours. (5) the table is made from two pieces of wood glued together. (6) and the candles are bits of straw stuck into press studs. (8) the divan is the remains of a little car. (9) the dresser is made up of bits of wood, bottle tops, little pieces of macaroni and a marble.

2 The rest of the furniture from the kitten house was made like this: (1) the shower is a paper cup with one side cut out. On the top there is a button glued to a hook. (2) the lavatory is a small square of polystyrene hollowed out in the middle, with a tiny helmet put in the hollow. (3) the bunk beds are made from two pieces of polystyrene joined together with orange sticks. (The ladder was part of a broken fire engine.) (4) the table is a strip of card folded into three. (5) the little table is a little round piece of polystyrene topped with a wooden disc. (6) the other table is a plastic cup cut in half. Then four legs were cut out of the plastic sides. (7) the divan is also a plastic cup with the sides shortened but instead of cutting out legs, the cup was turned upside down. Then it was cut in half vertically and was glued on to a piece of wood.

Furniture for the dolls' house made from a long box This is nearly all made from corks. This is what they are: (1) double bed (2) cupboard (3) bedside table (4) baby bath (5) cot (6) basin (7) fridge (8) washing machine (9) stove (10) kitchen sink (11) chairs (12) table (13) bookshelf (14) bath (15) lavatory (16) wash basin.

How to cut corks 1 Use a sharp knife (a penknife would do) and then cut little round slices, crosswise as though you were chopping radishes.

2 Be warned: it is easier to cut yourself than you would think. If you cut the corks lengthwise, you will get little oblongs.

3 The corks can also be cut in strips. You can now make any basic furniture you like.

Furniture for the dolls' house built with three squares of cardboard Here is most of the furniture in a line. You can see how to make the bed, table and cupboard only, because once you can do these, you can make any of the other things. For example, 1, 3, and 7 are made in exactly the same way as the bed; and 2, 8 and 9 can be made in the same way as the cupboard. The stools (5) are the only things which are different. They are little rolls of paper glued on to little paper squares. If you want to paint any of the furniture, you can do so. The wooden things look especially nice with a coat of varnish.

A corrugated cardboard bed 1 You can make a small bed or a cupboard like this. Cut out an oblong piece of corrugated cardboard.

2 Fold it as you can see in the photograph and fix the cardboard firmly into this shape with sticky tape. Now cut out another oblong of plain or corrugated cardboard.

3 This will be the head of the bed. Fix it with sticky tape to one end. You can cover the bed with whatever you want. A strip of coloured cotton, for example, looks pretty.

A paper table

1 Cut out a narrow strip of paper and fold it into three equal parts.

2 Now cut out the table legs. Make them wide enough so that the table will stand up, but don't cut as far as the fold, because this could spoil your table.

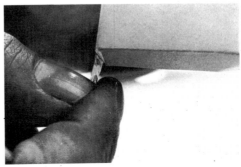

A paper cupboard 1 Find some squared paper and cut off the corners.

2 If you want to decorate your cupboard do that now. Now fold the paper into itself as you can see in the photograph.

3 Fix the four sides so that now you have a cupboard without a back. Cut out the door on three sides so that it will open and shut.

House mice

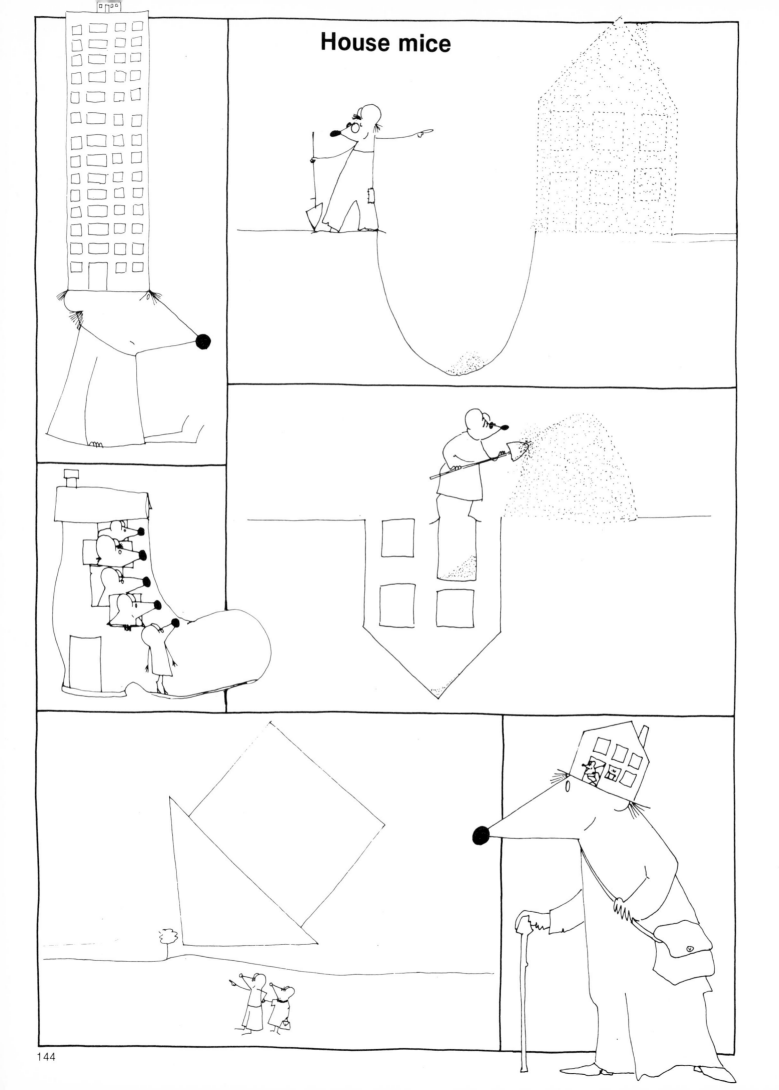

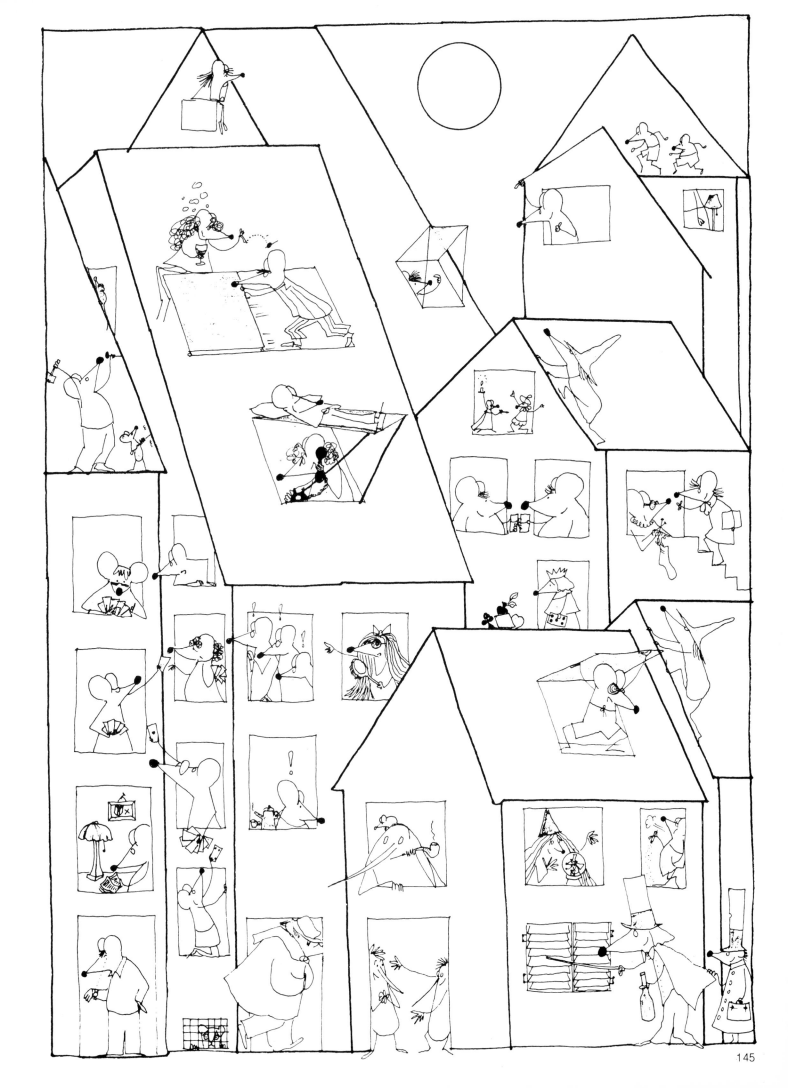

Kittens always turn up somewhere

Houses, villages, factories and schools; cats and dogs, castles and cities; rooms, huts, palaces, tents and towns, walls, games and models: there are lots of things in this book. If there had been the space, there would have been a whole lot more. So now it is up to you, if you were interested in anything, to look out for it in books and magazines. Being curious, and rooting out all sorts of strange and wonderful things about the world you live in is fun and maybe you find it that way already. Finding out about things doesn't begin and end with a book, of course. You can discover in many ways.

Now you have reached the last page, you could perhaps look back through this book. You might see something you hadn't noticed before. Above all, try to look at things in different ways and try to find out what you think yourself. Like this kitten. He has a mind of his own and he is always turning up where you don't expect him. I'll tell you what his name is. It's . . . no, you try and guess.

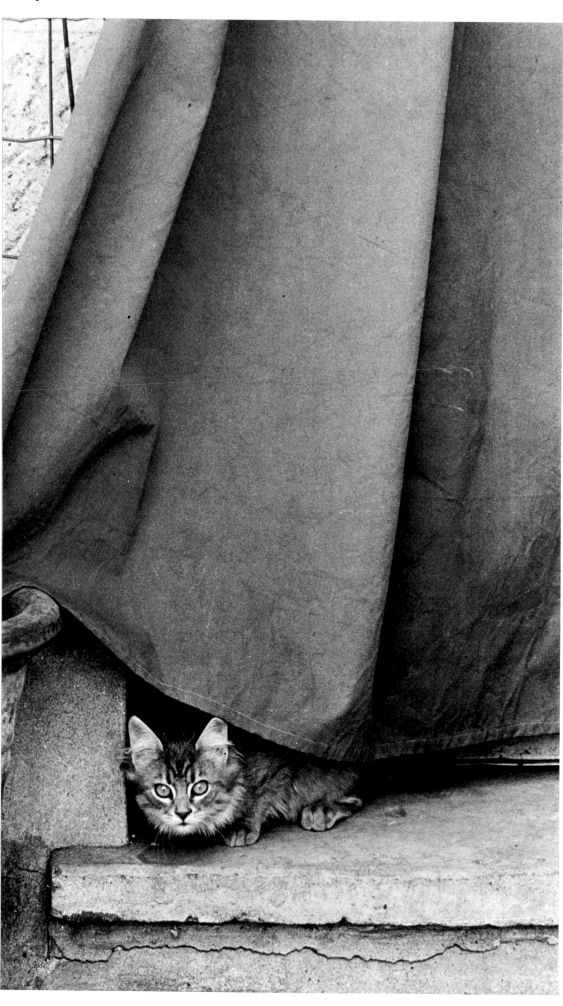

In this book

Summary of sections

Things to do

Stories and cartoons

General index

Index of artists and sources

Acknowledgements

The editors and publishers wish to record their grateful thanks to copyright owners for the use of illustrations listed below:

Agenzia Scala, Florence 50. Giorgio Anessi 86, *1*; 97, *10*. The archives of Emme Edizioni, Milan 72. The archives of the Consulate of the Federal Republic of Germany 26, *1*; 111, *5*. The archives of the Finnish Consulate 99, *6*. The archives of the French National Tourist Office 27, *8*; 29, *1*; 91, *4*. The archives of the Greek Tourist Office 61, *19*. The archives of IGDA/Air France 96, *3*. The archives of IGDA/Bevilacqua 60, *5*. The archives of IGDA/PubliAerfoto 88; 89; 96, *1*. The archives of the Japanese Consulate 26, *2*; 97, *7*; 110, *2*; 111, *4*. The archives of Mondadori 99, *7*. The archives of the Swiss National Tourist Office 26, *4*; 60. The archives of USIS 111, *1*. Enzo Arnone 59, *18*. Aldo Ballo 132, *4*. Gianni Gardin Berengo 70. Italo Bertolasi 58, *2*; 61, *13*; 80; 81; 110, *3*; 128, *8*. Baruch Bezner 29, *2*; 111, *3*. Paolo Carpi 30; 31; 39; 58, *3*; 60, *1, 7*; 62; 63; 64; 65; 78; 79; 96, *2*; 99, *9*; 111, *2*; 120; 133; 134; 135; 137; 138; 139; 140; 141; 142; 143; 146. Casali 132, *1, 5*. Valerio Castelli 11, *2*; 12, *2*; 18, *2, 3*; 19, *2*; 30, *2*; 37, *3*; 38, *1, 2, 3*; 58, *9, 13*; 59, *6, 7, 11, 16*; 60, *3, 6*; 61, *11, 14*; 84, *1, 2, 3*; 86, *2, 3*; 96, *4*; 98, *1*; 99, *5*; 110, *1*; 112; 127, *2*. CentroKappa 132, *3*. Ezio Colombo 14, *2*; 59, *8*. Deutsche Luftbild 90, *1*. Anselmo Fazzone 26, *3*. Alessandro Gogna 35, *3*; 51, *1, 2, 3, 4*. Carlo Leidi 102, *3*. Aldo Margiocco 118, *4*; 119, *5, 6, 7*. Bruno Mariette 58, *1*. Marina Molon 98, *3*. Jose Mondelo 14, *3*; 58, *10, 15*; 59, *5*. Daniele Pellegrini 18, *1*; 29, *3*; 118, *2, 3*. Mario Preti 93, *2, 3, 4*; 98, *4*; 99, *8*. Folco Quilici 10; 11, *2, 3*; 12, *1*; 13; 14, *1*; 15; 16; 17; 19, *1*; 27, *5, 6, 7, 9*; 30, *1*; 35, *2*; 36, *1*; 37, *2*; 58, *4*; 59, *12, 17*; 60, *9*; 61, *10, 12, 15, 16, 17, 18*; 68; 69; 71; 75; 76; 85; 90, *2*; 92, *1*; 94; 95; 96, *5*; 97, *6, 8, 9*; 102, *4*; 109; 114; 118, *1*; 127, *3, 5*; 128, *6*; 129; 139; *8, 9*. Paolo Riani 99, *10*. Matilde Rivolta 98, *2*. Laura Salvati 58, *14*; 60, *4, 8*; 73; 122; 124; 125; 126; 127, *4*; 128, *7*. Hermann Schlenker 77. Wilma Chiara Schultz 74. Emil Weiss 103, *5, 6, 7*. World Photo Service 91, *3*; 92, *2*.

The editors and publishers would also like to thank the children of the Scuola Elementare di Bosisio Parini and their headmaster, Nino Belgrano, who have given many helpful suggestions during the planning of this book as well as contributing drawings and paintings.

In addition we would like to thank the students of the Rione Traiano in Naples and architects Eduardo Alamaro and Anna Liguori for their permission to reproduce their plans for an experimental school; the children of the Scuola Elementare di Groppello and their teacher Joachino Maviglia; the children of the Scuola Elementare "La Vergine" di Pistoia and their teacher Giovanna Pelegatti; the children of the Scuola Elementare "A. Diaz" di Milano and their headmaster Maurizio Cottino; the children of the Scuola Elementare "G. Pascoli" (Milan) and their headmaster Bernardo Lilli; the children of the Scuola Elementare di via Manzoni di Trezzano sul Naviglio (Milan) and their teacher Maria Anastasi; the children of the Home d'Enfants "Les Gentiannes" in Crans sur Sierre (Switzerland) and their headmistress Mme Angèle Rey; the children and teachers of Circolo Didattico Ge-42, and the Comitato di Quartiere di Palmaro (Genoa). Special thanks go to G. Gandini for *House Mice*.

Finally, our grateful thanks for allowing us to use photographs in their possession listed below, go to architects Gambirasio, Ciaga and Zenoni for p. 102, *3*; professor Paolo Portoghesi for p. 93, *1* (taken from the book, *Horta*, Edizioni del Tritone, Rome 1969); *Architecture d'aujourd'hui* for p. 102, *1*; l'Instituto Italo-Cinese, Milan for p. 102, *2*; Gabriella Curiel, Uta Maiocchi and Giuliana Meda we would also like to thank for allowing us to photograph their dolls' houses.

For allowing their material to be reproduced in this book, thanks are also due to the following: Artemide of Milan; Kartell di Binasco (Milan); Zanotta of Milan.

A bit of bad luck by Jean Jacques Loup originally appeared as *Un architetto sfortunato*, and was taken from *L'architetto* published by Emme Edizioni, Milan 1976.

The white cat by Jorg Muller was taken from *Alle Jahre wieder saust der Presslufthammer nieder,* Sauerlander Verlag, Aarau.

Little Nemo in Slumberland by Winsor McCay was taken from *Little Nemo,* Nostalgia Press, New York.

Mr and Mrs Vinegar by Robert Nye is an extract from the story of the same name which appeared originally in *Once Upon Three Times*, published by Ernest Benn Limited, 1978.

Mr Kit E. Katte's house drawn by Pinin Carpi (p. 136) appeared originally as one of a series of posters called *J'apprends* © Edition Les Belles Images SARL.

I.G.D.A. Officine Grafiche, Novara - 1979 - Printed in Italy